Why Me?

Why Now?

What Now?

The Caregiving Years
Six Stages
to a Meaningful Journey

By Denise M. Brown

A Practical Field Guide to Create Your Map to Your Answers.

For more information and support, please visit Caregiving.com.

Thank you for buying our book! We also publish:
- *Take Comfort, Reflections of Hope for Caregivers;*
- *Take Comfort, Too, More Reflections of Hope for Caregivers;*
- *Take More Comfort, Reflectiosn of Hope for Caregivers;*
- *Take Even More Comfort, Reflections of Hope for Caregivers;*
- *Good Morning! Sunny Reflections to Start Your Day; and*
- *Take Time, a Journey and Journal Toward Greater Happiness During an Unhappy Time (Caregiving);*
- *My Caregiving Journal, My Story of How I Care;*
- *After Caregiving Ends, A Guide to Beginning Again.*

To purchase our books, please visit CareGiving.com.

Many thanks to Toni Gitles for her eagle-eye edits. You can connect with Toni, a Certified Caregiving Consultant and Educator, at www.heartlightenterprises.com.

The Caregiving Years, Six Stages to a Meaningful Journey, Eighth Edition
Copyright © 2018 Tad Publishing & Consulting Co. and Denise M. Brown

Published by Tad Publishing Co. and Consulting Co., Park Ridge, IL
773-343-6341 | www.caregiving.com

Published in the United States of America

ISBN: 978-1720425144 (Print)

To Mirca, in loving memory of an amazing mentor.

The Caregiving Years

Six Stages
to a Meaningful Journey

Parenting teaches you how to love.

Caregiving teaches you how to live.

"The road of life twists and turns and no two directions
are ever the same. Yet our lessons come from the journey,
not the destination." ~ Don Williams, Jr.

"To get through the hardest journey we need take only one step
at a time, but we must keep on stepping." ~ Chinese Proverbs

When you expect a child, the community (your family, friends, coworkers) rallies around you and your spouse. When you expect your first child, you receive gifts, well wishes and the encouragement that you are entering a wonderful, albeit challenging, chapter in your life. As you prepare to welcome your child, you feel pride at the thought of your role as parent: How you will shape the mind of a youngster, impacting him or her with your wisdom, insights and knowledge.

Now think about a similar life experience, one on the other end of the spectrum. When you care for a family member or friend, spending the last years together as caregiver and caree, you might feel isolated from the community. Friends, coworkers, even other relatives may say about your caregiving responsibilities: "I could never do that! Why do you?" Or, the more common response: "Why don't you just put your mother (or your wife, or your grandfather) in a nursing home? That way you won't be so stressed out."

With support like that, no wonder you might find yourself fighting self-doubts, asking yourself, "Why me? Why am I the one to do this?" These self-doubts can erode your ability to handle your caregiving responsibilities effectively and efficiently. Even worse, these self-doubts cloud your ability to understand how important this caregiving journey is--to your caree, your family, yourself.

That's why I've developed The Caregiving Years, Six Stages to a Meaningful Experience. Much like books for expecting parents, The Caregiving Years describes what to expect throughout the journey. Because no journey is completed without wrong turns, unexpected delays and unplanned crises (we'll call these "stumbles"), our map also includes ways to "steady" these stumbles.

Separated into six stages, The Caregiving Years reflects the increasing intensity of the caregiving role. Within each stage, you'll find a keyword. As you move through the stages, you'll add more keywords which also become your coping strategies. These six keywords become your go-to actions during times of stress, worry and frustration.

By having information about your role as family caregiver, as well as understanding the information needed and actions to take, you can spend more time making this experience meaningful for your caree, your family and yourself.

"You can't stay in your corner of the Forest waiting for others to come to you. You have to go to them sometimes."
~ Winnie the Pooh

"You are braver than you believe, stronger than you seem and smarter than you think." ~ Christopher Robin

Stage I:
The Expectant Caregiver

*In the future, I may help
a family member or friend.*

Who are you?

You have a growing concern that, within the near future, a family member or friend will need more and more of your assistance and time. You're concerned because of your relative's age, past and present medical condition, and current living condition.

Your keyword: Ask

--Ask questions of your caree. (The individual receiving your care is your "caree.")
--Ask questions of health care professionals.
--Ask questions of lawyers and financial planners.
--Ask questions of your family members who may be involved in the caregiving role.

Your Challenge

To learn and understand your caree's needs: health, financial, legal and emotional.

Your Purpose

You expect to become a caregiver; this is your time to prepare. You can research options, gather information, and provide the opportunity for your caree to share his or her feelings and values. This is also your time to concentrate on taking care of yourself--keeping up with family and friends, enjoying your hobbies and interests, pursuing your career goals.

The Family Caregivers and Carees
Judy and Frank

Judy has worried about her husband, Frank, since his retirement five years ago. It seems that once he stopped working, he sat in his recliner and never moved except to refill his beer and light up his cigar. Once a vibrant, competitive, intelligent man, Frank now just seems like a heart attack or stroke just waiting to happen. No words of encouragement from her, their children or Frank's doctor have been able to get him up and off the couch.

Frank's doctor has warned that unless Frank gives up the cigars and alcohol and begins a regular exercise program, Frank is doomed to be a victim of his unhealthy lifestyle choices.

Judy can see what's in her future: a husband who will need her full-time care.

Andy and Abigail

Andy and his mother, Abigail, have always been close. Although they live across the country from each other (Andy in Denver and Abigail in Brooklyn in the same home Andy grew up in), they still remain as close as ever. Daily telephone conversations make the distance seem no more than a few city blocks.

Abigail is nearing 80 years old. Andy counts his blessing that his mother has been healthy and independent most of her life. Andy has noticed some subtle changes in his mother's routine. Getting to the grocery store every week seems to tire his mother. Cooking and baking seems to interest his mother less and less and his mother relies more and more on frozen dinners. Outings with friends to Atlantic City to play the slots have become fewer and fewer. Abigail is slowing down. Andy knows that the change in his mother's abilities and condition could very well change his mother's living situation.

Andy has two siblings who moved away from Brooklyn, just as Andy did. Their move became as much emotional as physical. They rarely keep in touch with either Andy or Abigail.

Although an immediate crisis does not face Judy or Andy, the threat of one seems to hang in the horizon. Rather than closing their eyes to avoid seeing that horizon, Judy and Andy can take some proactive steps now that will make their future caregiving days easier.

As an "expectant caregiver," what can you do?
1. Consult with a good lawyer familiar with caregiving issues.
Find out about durable powers of attorney for finances and health care as well as living wills; start the process to ensure your caree has the necessary legal papers in order. Ask the attorney: What do we need to know to be prepared for the future? What additional documents will we need? What should we keep in mind?

A durable power of attorney for finances and health care appoints an agent to make decisions on behalf of your caree when he or she is unable to. If you live in one state and your caree in another, ask an elderlaw attorney about creating documents for both states in case you move your caree to your area in the future.

A Stumble: Judy assumes Frank won't want to discuss important issues about his death, his funeral and their will.

A Steady: Wouldn't you want to the opportunity to tell your family members how you want to die? What kind of funeral do you envision? Allowing Frank to share this information now will be a relief to both Judy and Frank in the future. Judy will be able to confidently make decisions about Frank's care treatments and care plans.

2. Determine financial situations.
Knowing the financial status of your caree can help determine future health care choices. Determine monthly income from pensions and social security; learn about annuities, stock investments and bank accounts. Meet with financial planners to understand how to ensure investments last as long as possible. Learn where passwords for online accounts are kept.

A Stumble: Your caree refuses your request to disclose financial information.

A Steady: If your caree won't disclose particulars about his or her financial situation, be sure to at least know at which banks he or she has accounts and where important papers can be found.

3. Investigate community health care options.
For Judy, what home health care agencies in her area offer quality, affordable home care? For Andy, what housing options are available for Abigail-- retirement communities, assisted living centers? Contact community organizations to request brochures and pamphlets and research these organizations online.
   In addition, consider your caree's current living condition. Will your caree be able to reside safely in her home if she uses a wheelchair or becomes bed-bound? What changes can you make today that will prevent future barriers to providing care in her home? Or are the necessary changes almost an impossibility? If so, what other options do you have, such as your home, an assisted living facility, a retirement community?

4. Determine the current health care providers.
Judy will be familiar with her husband's physician. Andy can learn as much as possible about his mother's physician. In addition, he can learn about his mother's medications and why the medications have been prescribed.

5. Get organized.
Before you know it, you'll be surrounded by paperwork. Put your house in order so that you'll be ready to manage your caree's financial, legal and medical information. Project management tools like Trello (trello.com) will be helpful now and going forward when you manage caregiving, one of life's greatest projects.

6. Understand your family member's routine.
When does he or she get up in the morning? Go to bed? How often does he or she attend the local senior center, library or worship services? Who does he or she call on a regular basis? Who are the friends he or she enjoys? When you understand the routine, you'll notice when problems occur that may need your intervention. In the future, if a move takes place, you can re-create the routine to provide comfort.

7. Concentrate on the reality of the situations.
Both Judy and Andy can keep a realistic view of their situation. What's the worst that could happen? What's the best possible outcome? Next, determine which options are available for each of these outcomes. For instance, if Abigail is no longer able to live on her own, is it realistic for Andy to consider moving back to Brooklyn to be closer to his mother? For Judy, is it in her best interest to stay at home and watch Frank on his collision course with a health disaster? Would it be better for her to develop her own friends and interests?

A Stumble: Believing that nothing could possibly happen to you or your caree. As such, you believe finding this type of information is unnecessary and a waste of time.

A Steady: Understanding that information is power. The more you know about your caree's medical condition, financial situation and the community options, the better and more informed your future decisions about your caree's care will be.

8. Start a journal to chronicle your feelings, your concerns and your actions.
You may be surprised at feelings of loss. Your preparation of the future allows you to see what your caree and you might lose. You both will experience changes in your relationship, your schedules, your amount of freedom. Write down your thoughts about the potential losses--and how you might be able to hang on to them, through minor adjustments and changes, for a little longer.

9. Take time to sort out your own issues.
It's easy to overlook these issues when life seems easy. Caregiving, especially as it intensifies, will make life hard. It's harder if you have unresolved emotional work as it relates to your caree or other family members. For instance, Judy can work with a social worker or therapist to manage any resentment she may feel toward her husband. Andy can make contact with his siblings to let them know of his concerns. If they choose to keep their distance, Andy can touch base with a therapist or life coach to create a plan for future communication with his siblings.
   If you have difficulty standing up for yourself or finding your voice, this is a good time to work with a therapist or life coach to gain confidence in expressing your needs and using your voice to share your concerns.
   When do you struggle with the idea of asking for help? Now is a good time to figure out why and start practicing. Knowing how and when to ask for help is a great skill, which will become a huge asset for you.
   The Four Agreements, A Practical Guide to Personal Freedom, a book by Don Miguel Ruiz, offers insights about our personal codes of conduct. As your caregiving journey continues, you'll interact with family, friends and health care professionals who will drive you nuts. This book will give you the tools so you can stay sane.

10. Find your best shape—physically, emotionally and financially.
Find a work-out routine you like. Maximize the amount of healthy foods you eat. Pay off your debts. Save as much as you can. Uncomfortable managing money? Read books and take classes online and in your community to become comfortable. You'll need to be at your best—physically, emotionally and financially.

11. Learn your caree's life story.
Document the story in a journal, video or audio recording. Collect recipes, photos, letters, poems and records that reflect your caree's life and

achievements. Ask questions about your caree's childhood, parents, siblings and first loves. Involve other family members, including children, in the discussions.

12. Ask your caree to introduce you to those individuals he or she values. Ask to meet with your caree's financial planners, attorneys, physicians, minister or rabbi and other important professionals in his or her life. The relationship you form now will help you make good decisions and take effective steps later.

13. Begin each day with the knowledge that you have love.
Perhaps the toughest battles in caregiving begin within. Most battles really are about whether or not you are loved. That doubt begins the chase to find the love. End the running now. You are loved. Know it now so you can remind yourself later.

14. An apple a day…
What can you do on a regular basis to keep yourself healthy? Be good to yourself—you are too important today and tomorrow and every day after that to let your own health slip. In other words, what's your apple?

A Quick Tip:
Attempts to begin discussions about difficult conversations can leave us sputtering and our caree spitting. It's okay. It may take a few times to begin such a discussion. If you feel completely overwhelmed by the thought of such a discussion, enlist the help of a trusted, objective third party, such as a physician, clergy or rabbi, or another family member.

Have you completed your own important legal documents? If not, that's a great way to start the discussion with your caree. Suggest you both meet with an attorney to complete your durable powers of attorney, advance directives and wills.

Lastly, simple is your friend. Think of a simple way to start the conversation even by saying, "I have no idea how to ask you about something that's very important to me. Please be patient with me. I'm a little nervous."

As your journey continues, keep in mind the simple solutions. Caregiving is complicated, which is why it calls for simplicity.

The Expectant Caregiver
Your Reflections

Who might need your care in the future? What questions can you ask now?

Who might provide care for you in the future? What information can you share now?

In this stage, what are your goals?
—For your current caree? For a potential future caree?

—For you and your family?

How will you achieve these goals?

Who can help you achieve these goals?

What are your worries?
—For your caree?

—For you and your family?

How can you overcome these worries?

The Expectant Caregiver
Your Resource Library

Your Must Knows

When you begin to care for a family member or friend, you find yourself in a completely foreign land. It feels like you immediately need to know how to speak the language in this land.

But, how can you? You didn't expect to be here, you didn't receive training on how to manage here and you certainly didn't receive a map once you arrived.

We've compiled some must-know tips to help.

1. **Medicare is not Medicaid and vice versa**. Medicare, the federal insurance program typically for person's 65 and over, has very limited benefits to cover long-term care needs, either in a home or in a nursing home. Medicaid, a state-funded program typically for low-income persons, pays for the costs of in-home and nursing home care as long as a caree's income is low enough to qualify for benefits.

2. Caregiving will cost you. According to a 2017 Caring.com report, **44% of respondents spend at least $5,000 annually to care for their loved ones, with 25% spending $10,000 and more**. An AARP study, "Family Caregiving and Out-of-Pocket Costs: 2016 Report," estimates that family caregivers spend an average of $6,954 on out-of-pocket costs related to caregiving, nearly 20 percent of their annual income.

For the most recent data on costs of nursing homes, assisted living facilities, home health agencies and adult day programs, check Genworth's Cost of Care at www.genworth.com/aging-and-you/finances/cost-of-care.html

3. You can **appeal decisions that discontinue Medicare coverage** in a nursing home or hospital or home health. The nursing home, hospital or home health agency will provide you with information on how to appeal. If they don't, ask.

4. **Watch how health care professionals provide care** to your caree. Before a hospital discharge, tape any training the professionals provide to you. Tape the training at home when a home health aide provides care. And,

always makes sure a health care professional washes their hands and wear gloves whenever they provide care.

5. **Check and then double check information you receive**. Sometimes, health care professionals share correct information. Sometimes, they don't. It's worth the repeat phone calls to confirm you have the right details.

6. **Know the good home health agencies, nursing homes, adult day centers and assisted living facilities in your community** and your caree's if you live in different areas. You may need these providers for short-term help (like recovery after a caree's broken hip after a fall) or respite care (so you can take a break) or long-term (when care at home becomes too difficult). Ask your caree's doctor for referrals and ask friends for their recommendations. Be in the know because you just never know.

7. **Check Medicare-certified providers at Medicare's rating website: www.medicare.gov.** Medicare rates the quality of care provided by hospitals, home health agencies, nursing homes, dialysis centers, health and drug programs, and equipment suppliers. Their data can help you make the best decision possible.

8. **Research the impact of transferring your caree's assets**, including the home, so that you do not incur penalties or jeopardize Medicaid benefits.

9. **If you are a caregiving adult child living with your caree in your caree's home**, your caree could transfer the home to you without jeopardizing Medicaid benefits. Check with an elderlaw attorney to learn more.

10. If you care for a spouse, know that some assets must be protected for you through the **Spousal Impoverishment program**. Check Medicaid.gov for details.

11. **Hospitals have ethics committees** which can help you if you face a tough decision if your family can't agree on a decision.

12. **Watch the caregiving budget**, taking into account care needs and the reality of your caree remaining at home. It's easier to find a good nursing home when your caree can pay privately for at least one year. It's really

tough to find a good facility that has availability when your caree is on Medicaid.

13. **Always ask if a nursing home or assisted living facility accepts Medicaid**. If your caree moves to a facility that doesn't accept Medicaid and your caree runs out of money, your caree will have to move. You'll want to avoid a move as much as possible.

14. **The best day to look for support is on a good day and early in your caregiving experience**. When you create your support on a good day, it will be there for you on a bad day. There's nothing worse than trying to drive to a new support group or decide to start a blog on a day when you are too stressed to think clearly. You'll need support. Find it and nurture it on your good days. Use it on your difficult ones.

15. Prepare for the long haul–**caregiving lasts longer than you'll imagine or expect**.

16. **Own it**. If you silently hope someone else will say the hard words, make the difficult decisions, take the awful actions, then you'll waste time that could lead to chaos. Others will follow your silent lead, which means no one else will say the hard words, make the difficult decisions, take the awful actions. It's terrible that it falls on you. But, you can make the situation a little better by saying the hard words, making the difficult decisions and taking the awful action. Take the deep breath and do it.

17. **If your caree is over 60 years of age, call your local Area Agency on Aging** to find out about programs and services which may help both of you. Find your local Area Agency on Aging at eldercare.gov. You also can search for help at benefits.gov and benefitscheckup.org.

18. **If you care for a veteran**, check www.caregiver.va.gov or call 1-855-260-3274 about programs and services to help you.

19. **If you care for a family member with dementia**, call the Alzheimer's Association 24-hour hot line at 1-800-272-3900 for support and help.

20. **If you work**, check with your employer about an Employee Assistance Program, which may have programs and services to help.

21. **The Family Medical Leave Act allows you to take up to 12 weeks unpaid time off each year** for specified family and medical reasons. You can take 12 weeks at once or split up the unpaid leave over days, weeks or months.

22. **Find the disease specific organizations and associations** (like the Alzheimer's Association, American Stroke Association, Michael J. Fox Foundation) to connect to support and help for both you and your caree.

23. **You will struggle to find help, to be understood and to feel like you belong.** It's an awful struggle. As much as you can, avoid taking it personally. Let it hurt, then move on. Moving on will help you climb out of the struggle. You will find help, you are understood and you do belong.

24. **Document your caree's needs, doctor's appointments, medications, medical conditions in a spreadsheet or an app like Evernote.** You'll be able to search the spreadsheet or app when you need to know when your caree started a certain med, for instance, or the reason for the last hospitalization.

25. **Understand end-of-life** so you'll understand what's happening during your caree's end of life. National Institute on Aging has helpful end-of-life guides; visit www.nia.nih.gov.

Why End-of-Life Conversations Matter

Geri, who cares for her husband, shared a difficult story about her mother-in-law's death. Her mother-in-law spent her last 10 weeks of life in the hospital, three and half weeks longer than her two sons wanted. She hadn't made her wishes known, so her husband did everything and more to keep her alive. Her last weeks were painful and difficult as her husband agonized over letting go because he didn't know when she wanted him to let go.

After she died, the family struggled to make arrangements, simply because they weren't sure of her wishes.

Over the years, Geri and her husband, Barry, tried to talk to her in-laws about their wishes. She writes:

"Barry and I have tried to talk to his parents about this for years. I appealed to my father-in-law from a financial angle that it will be less expensive to make your arrangements in advance. I appealed to him from an emotional angle by asking, Do you want your wife to be making these decisions in her darkest hour? Barry took a tougher stance and threatened to bury them in the yard with the cats."

When the conversations about end-of-life stay one-sided, what can you do? Some suggestions:

1. **Try, take a break and try again.** The process of gathering the necessary information about finances, end-of-life decisions and final arrangements can be one that lasts years.

2. **Do your best and when you hit a brick wall, respect a caree's decision not to share.** You can only do your best. You can express your worry ("I worry I won't do what you'll want") and if that doesn't work, then let it go for the time being. Then, try again at a later date.

3. **If you can't get specifics, then get generalities.** If you are unsure of a caree's financial situation and your caree insists it's none of your business, then ask where the banking happens, for contact information for financial planners and where important paperwork can be found.

4. **Try to make it a family affair.** Schedule a meeting for everyone to talk about their wishes. You can use a workbook like *Five Wishes*, which documents your wishes if you become seriously ill, to spark the discussion. With everyone sharing, the focus isn't just on your caree. It's never too soon to know about family members' wishes, regardless of age. (See below for details about *Five Wishes*.)

5. **Ask about their experiences.** How did their parents (your grandparents) manage as they aged? How did their families manage caregiving? What rituals and traditions did your caree participate in when family members died? The past can give you clues about how to manage the future.

6. **You can try the "I'm assuming" tactic.** "Dad, I'm assuming you want to be buried with Mom. I'm also assuming you want a wake and funeral. Is this correct?" "Mom, I'm assuming you want to be cremated like Aunt Alice. Is this correct?" And, "Dad, I'm assuming you haven't made any plans for your funeral and burial. Is this correct?"

Resources for End-of-Life Conversations
- The Conversation Project: The Conversation Project helps people talk about their wishes for end-of-life care. www.theconversationproject.org
- Engage with Grace: The One Slide Project was designed with one simple goal: to help get the conversation about the end-of-life experience started. The idea is simple: Create a tool to help get people talking. One Slide has just five questions designed to help get us talking with each other and with our loved ones about our preferences. www.engagewithgrace.org
- Five Wishes: Five Wishes helps you express how you want to be treated if you are seriously ill and unable to speak for yourself. It deals with all of a person's needs, including medical, personal, emotional and spiritual. www.fivewishes.org
- Prepare: PREPARE is a program that can help you make medical decisions for yourself and others; talk with your doctors; and get the medical care that is right for you. www.prepareforyourcare.org

The 3 Be's of Caregiving

Caregiving conundrums will be a part of your caregiving experience; to help you stay on track we've developed The Three Be's of Caregiving: Be Prepared, Be Honest and Be Well. To help you look at your Three Be's, we've developed the following questions to ask yourself:

Be Prepared:
- What does the future hold for your caree? What will his or her care needs be? What community services are available to provided the needed care? If in-home will not meet the care needs, which housing options will?
- What can your caree afford in terms of care? If budget restrictions are a concern, what other community programs or services (or state or federal) programs can offset the costs of care?
- What information or training do you need to be a qualified, effective caregiver? Where can you gather the information or learn the caregiving techniques?

Be Honest:
- What are your limits as a caregiver? Can family members, friends or community services fill those voids? If not, what other options are available?
- How long can you afford emotionally, financially and physically in order to provide care in your home or in your caree's home?

Be Well:
- What interests and hobbies are important to you? How can you maintain these?
- How can you find time to relax even for a few moments?
- How can you integrate a fitness program into your routine?
- How can you maintain a regular support system?
- How can you release all those negative emotions of caregiving in a healthy way?
- How can you better express your feelings and your beliefs so that family members and friends understand your goals as a caregiver?
- In what areas do you need help? How can you get that help?
- In what ways can you bring joy and laughter into your life and your caree's on a regular basis?

The Planning

(I published the following blog post on CareGiving.com on Jan. 23, 2018. I share as a reminder our discussions about wishes remains a process.)

My mom fell on Sunday morning at 7:30 a.m. My dad called me at 7:40 a.m., casually asking what I had going on during the day. "I have a training today," I explained, biting my tongue when I wanted to say, "Remember? I have a training."

"What time does that start," he asked.

"9," I replied, followed by, "What's going on, Dad?"

"Well, your mother fell."

"Where is she now?"

"On the floor."

"When did she fall?"

"10 minutes ago."

"I'll be right there."

When I arrived, my mom was sitting on the floor. A gash above the goose egg above her eye was bleeding and my dad had piled up wash clothes with blood on them on the table. I suggested she go the ER. "I'm concerned you have an internal contusion which will burst and you will die," I explained not quite correctly or with much sensitivity but wanted to get the point across. I cleaned her up as we continued to discuss the ER.

Ultimately, they decided against it, which I was okay with. I offer the suggestions, participate in discussions around the decision and then honor their decisions. I don't want to withhold information ("and you will die") which I believe they need to make a decision that's right for them. I then called my younger sister to relieve me so I could get to my training. Unfortunately, my mom has been falling for several years but the sight of her with facial bruising and a black eye is still jolting. I feel like I watch my parents fade — it's not a sudden disappearance but a slow and steady one. I know what's coming.

Because I know what's coming, I've started the conversation about their funeral plans a few times over the years. I began about seven years ago while driving my mom to an appointment. She shared about a funeral she had just attended so I walked through the open door and asked about her preferences. "Oh, do whatever you want," she said. "I won't be here."

I tried again after that dead-end conversation during a visit with other family members, including a sibling and brother-in-law. I shared my wishes and asked about what others wanted. My parents got up from the living room and headed into the kitchen in the middle of our discussion. Door closed.

I began 2016 with a determined goal to learn the funeral plans. During a lunch with my parents when they lived in the retirement community, I asked about funeral plans. The lunch happened to be to celebrate my birthday, so my dad said, "Do we really have to do this now?' and then my mom started throwing up. My mom was recovering from surgery to remove a 1/3 of her stomach to stop an internal bleed and sometimes threw up after eating a dish too rich or sweet. 2016 and 2017 both closed without any funeral plans in place.

So, yesterday, during a visit to make sure they are doing okay, I said to my parents, "I'd like to meet your financial planner just so he knows who I am," I said. I had the idea to do this on Saturday during a presentation by Toni Gitles, a student in the weekend's Certified Caregiving Consultant and Educator training programs. Toni delivered a presentation focused on preparing for caregiving during which I had an ah-ha! moment. I know who my parents use to manage their money and I've met him socially during a church event. Actually meeting him to discuss how to contact him after my parents' death seemed like a good idea.

My parents agreed with my request and my reasoning. My dad immediately made an appointment for us to meet with the financial planner. With the success of that suggestion, I tackled the funeral plans again. This time, my mom had special requests. Hearing hers led my dad to share his. Interestingly enough, they each want a different funeral home, which I have duly noted. They still need to decide if they want to be cremated or buried and are debating which restaurant to suggest for the luncheon after their funeral masses. As they discussed restaurant options, they both pulled out their iPhones to review menus and pricing for local restaurants.

We had a bit of a crash on Sunday morning. Yesterday, after calm and thoughtful conversations, we've found our footing.

Do We Need a POA for Love?

Several years ago, Dick, who cared for his wife with Alzheimer's until her death, moderated the men's online support group for me on CareGiving.com. He was close to 90 and fun, witty and caring. He was a catch.

Genie thought so, too. She met Dick in a support group for persons caring for a family member with Alzheimer's. Her husband resided in an assisted living facility. Dick, now widowed, and Genie, whose husband lived in a facility, began dating. Then they fell in love.

I'm not sure if I struggled with this relationship because Genie was still married or simply because I didn't like Genie (I found her a bit unkind when they paid me a visit). Genie's five adult sons were adamantly opposed to the relationship. Dick and Genie moved in together, although kept up the appearance of separate residences because of her sons. Then, Genie was diagnosed with a brain tumor. Dick cared for her until her death a few months after her diagnosis.

That turn of events made me think that maybe I'm not in any kind of position to judge what's right or wrong.

More and more family caregivers are sharing their stories of dating and falling in love with someone other than their spouse. Consider Barry Petersen, a CBS News correspondent, who cared for his wife, Jan, who had Alzheimer's and resided in an assisted living facility. Barry openly talked about dating Mary Nell in a segment that aired on *CBS This Morning*.

"Together, we visit Jan, and together we watch over her," Petersen said during the segment. "Mary Nell understood from the beginning that ours is a relationship of three because it will always include Jan, the woman Mary Nell now calls her friend."

Then there's the case of 82-year-old Dorothy and 95-year-old Bob, who met in a nursing home and were profiled in a 2008 Slate.com article called "An Affair to Remember." Ten years after first reading the article, I'm still haunted by what happened to them. Dorothy's arrival at the facility where Bob lived turned Bob from a player into Dorothy's devoted boyfriend.

Both had dementia. They also exhibited all the signs of two people in love. They started to do what people in love do—they had sex. It also sounds like they had sex as often as they could.

It all went downhill after that. Bob's son, the power of attorney, disapproved. When he demanded that Bob and Dorothy be separated, Dorothy lost 21 pounds, was hospitalized for dehydration and treated for depression. She had all the symptoms of a broken heart.

Ultimately, Bob's son moved his father to another facility. He did not allow Bob and Dorothy a chance to say good-bye to each other.

I tell these stories, and others, in a seminar I deliver called "What's Love Got to Do With It?" During the presentation, I discuss how caregiving and long-term illnesses affect marriages and our definitions of fidelity and commitment.

Each time I've given the presentation, an attendee has said, "Maybe we should discuss these issues like we discuss our wishes for our care at end of life. Maybe we also need to appoint a durable power of attorney for love in addition to one for health care and finances."

In her Slate.com article about Bob and Dorothy, Melinda Henneberger writes, "And if we get lucky when we're old, then we need to have drawn up a sexual power of attorney before it's too late. Who controls the intimate lives of people with dementia?"

During one of my presentations, an attendee shared her story. Her mother, diagnosed with dementia, resides in a nursing home. Her father now dates another woman. The daughter is devastated by this. "It's just so hard," she said. She speaks with her sister about the situation but not with her father.

Perhaps, if we needed to appoint a POA for love, then we also would discuss dating during caregiving. Perhaps the seminar attendee's parents would have talked about the "what if" scenario. "What if I no longer know who you are? Will you want to date? I'm okay (or not okay) with this if you do." If the daughter knew that her mother would be okay with her father dating, then would this knowledge comfort her today? If the mother had expressed different wishes, well, then, would the husband have chosen a different course of action? If the daughter knew her mother did not want her father to date and then her father did, would this have given the daughter the courage to speak up and discuss her concerns with her father, to voice how upsetting she found the situation?

If Bob and Dorothy each had a durable POA for love, then would they have had a better chance to enjoy their love story? Would the POA for love have respected their mutual love and recognized that a diagnosis of dementia meant they forgot names but not how to feel and express love?

When we have conversations about future wishes, let's ask about love. We all need it and want it, no matter our diagnosis or age. It's important we understand how our family members and friends want love to remain for the rest of their lives. It's just as important that they understand how we want love to live for us.

Your Care Plan:
Your Plan for What You Want and Need

You hear this all the time: When you care for another, you have to take care of yourself.

The problem is that no one ever tells you exactly how to do this. How in the world, when your world is full of too much to do with too few hands and too little time, do you take care of yourself?

You just need a plan. Just like your caree has a plan of care, so do you.

I've created a care plan which you can use to create a weekly plan.

In our care plan, we define WELL this way:

- Wisdom comes from being attentive grateful and curious.
- Energy comes from your food, your exercise and your breaks.
- Laughter comes from within, from your relationships and from your entertainment.
- Love comes from within, from your relationships and from your passions.

And, to keep you from falling into the well, you'll also add thoughts in your care plan about forgiving yourself, family members, friends, your caree, the disease process and whatever else causes you pain and sorrow. Because forgiveness is a work in progress, you also can include comments on where you are in the process.

To help you complete your care plan, I've also included an example of a completed care plan.

In addition, you can hire a Certified Caregiving Consultant to help you complete your plan and keep you accountable to your plan.

My Care Plan

My care plan focuses on my **WELL**:

- Wisdom comes from being attentive, grateful and curious.
- Energy comes from my food, my exercise and my physical, mental, spiritual and emotional breaks.
- Laughter comes from within myself, from my relationships and from my entertainment.
- Love comes from within myself, from my relationships and from my passions.

And, to keep me from falling into the well, I'll also focus on forgiveness of myself, family members, friends, my caree, the disease process and whatever else causes me pain and sorrow. I also recognize that forgiveness is a work in progress.

During the week, I make the following commitments to staying **WELL**:

I stay attentive to:

I am grateful for:

I am curious about:

My food choices include:

My exercise routine is:

My Care Plan

I take breaks:
- for my body:
- for my mind:
- for my spirit:
- for my heart:

I laugh about:

I laugh with:

I laugh while:

I love when I:

I love:

I love participating in these activities:

I forgive:

I am working on forgiving:

My Care Plan
for the Week of May 6, 2018

My care plan focuses on my **WELL**:

- **W**isdom comes from being attentive, grateful and curious.
- **E**nergy comes from my food, my exercise and my physical, mental, spiritual and emotional breaks.
- **L**aughter comes from within myself, from my relationships and from my entertainment.
- **L**ove comes from within myself, from my relationships and from my passions.

And, to keep me from falling into the well, I'll also focus on forgiveness of myself, family members, friends, my caree, the disease process and whatever else causes me pain and sorrow. I also recognize that forgiveness is a work in progress.

During the week of May 6, I make the following commitments to staying **WELL**:

I stay attentive to: *my bed time, so I get enough sleep*

I am grateful for: *all those who help me*

I am curious about: *how individuals overcome tough personal situations so I'll ask the librarian for suggestions on good autobiographies*

My food choices include: *peanut butter on whole grain toast at 10 a.m., salads for lunch and fruit for a 3 p.m. salad. Dinner will include the foods I love.*

My exercise routine is: *a 30-minute walk after dinner five times a week*

My Care Plan

I take breaks:

for my body: *I'll take a break to enjoy music each afternoon to give my body a rest*

for my mind: *I'll take a break from my worries by working on my vision board on Sunday afternoon*

for my spirit: *I'll begin each day with five minutes of meditation*

for my heart: *I'll connect with other family caregivers at least once a day to share and support*

I laugh about: *the funny moments in my day*

I laugh with: *my friends whenever I can*

I laugh while: *I watch my TV shows, especially Modern Family*

I love when I: *stand up for what I need and speak my mind*

I love: *my family members and friends*

I love participating in these activities: *reading and writing so will make time for each every day*

I forgive: *myself for being impatient and my sister for not being able to help*

I am working on forgiving: *myself for past decisions. To help me with this process, I'll journal for a few moments about those past decisions.*

Signed: *Denise M. Brown*   Date: *May 6, 2018*

"One does not have to stand against the gale.
One yields and becomes part of the wind." - Emmanuel

"It's not the load that breaks you down,
it's the way you carry it." ~ Lena Horne

Stage II:
The Freshman Caregiver

I am starting to help a family member or friend.

Who are you?
You've begun to help your family member on a regular basis, weekly, perhaps even a few times a week. Your duties range from errand-running and bill-paying to some assistance with hands-on care.

Your keyword: Find
--Find services that help.
--Find a system that keeps you organized.
--Find support that comforts.
--Find ways to enjoy your hobbies and interest.

Your Challenge
To discover solutions that work and to feel comfortable moving on from what doesn't.

Your Purpose
This is your entry into the caregiving role. This is your time to experiment, to get your feet wet and see what works. This is your opportunity to learn how the health care industry works with, or in some cases against, you. Now is the time to shape your caregiving personality. What duties are you comfortable with? What duties make you uncomfortable? How well are you and your caree getting along? What situations would create overwhelming stresses for both of you?

   This is also the time when you get a feel for the present and future budgets needed to provide the care your caree requires.

   In addition, keep up with your hobbies and interests (you may be able only to keep the ones that you enjoy most), ensuring you have made a habit of spending time on your own, enjoying yourself.

Judy and Frank
Just as his physician predicted, Frank suffered a series of strokes that have left him paralyzed on one side. Now, Judy helps bathe, dress and feed her husband. Frank suffered his first stroke 13 months ago, almost one year after Judy consulted with an eldercare attorney and their accountant.

Andy and Abigail

Abigail fell in her home and broke her hip eight months ago. After a short-term stay in a nursing home for rehab, Abigail has returned home--for now. Andy has arranged for Meals on Wheels to deliver daily meals. A home health aide visits twice a week to bathe Abigail as well as do the laundry and light grocery shopping. Andy has begun to discuss alternative housing with his mother. He shares his concern that the house has become too much of a burden for Abigail. He asks his mother, "How long do you want to live in the house? What other options you would consider?" Andy, who took a week off work to help his mother when she first returned home from the nursing home, plans a trip home for a long weekend to discuss options with his mother.

Andy continues to update his siblings with email messages. His siblings continue to choose to be uninvolved.

As a "freshman caregiver," what can you do?

1. Learn as much as you can about your caree's illness, disease or condition.

Consult the local branches or chapters of national organizations such as The Arthritis Foundation, the Alzheimer's Association, The Cancer Society. What does the future hold for you and your caree?

2. Learn how to provide proper care from health care professionals or from health care videos, manuals or books.

If your caree is hospitalized or receives short-term therapy at a nursing home, ask the staff to show you proper caregiving techniques: lifting, transfers, bathing. If you can, record the therapy sessions so you can refer to your videos when you're providing the care at home. Or, search the Internet, including YouTube, for hands-on care information and tutorials.

It's very difficult to provide care when you are unsure of what you're doing. You'll feel much better when you're confident of your skills.

A Stumble: During the discharge process from the nursing home to home, the social worker quickly explains Medicare benefits that will cover Abigail's rehab at a local skilled nursing facility. Three weeks later, Abigail receives a notice that Medicare will no longer cover her stay. Both Abigail and Andy are taken off guard--they thought Medicare benefits were available as long as Abigail needed them. They had not budgeted to pay for services privately.

A Steady: A hurried explanation from a health care professional about insurance coverage, care treatments or follow-up appointments can mean miscommunication and misunderstanding, creating the potential for future disasters. If the health care professional is hurried during any discussion with you, ask if you can contact her at a better time to discuss the information in greater detail. In addition, ask for any explanations regarding insurance coverage in writing.

3. Join a support group online or in your community.
It's so isolating to be a family caregiver! Support groups will hook you up with others in similar situations; often, you'll learn of community resources and options from other caregivers that you were not aware of.

4. Count on regular breaks from caregiving.
Plan for regular breaks--an hour daily, an afternoon weekly, or a day monthly--whatever you can manage. Enlist the help of relatives and community services (such as a volunteer group at your local church) so you can take time off regularly. Relatives might be able to help in several ways--through financial support, social support (calling the caree regularly just "to talk") as well as respite support.

   You may think, "Oh, this isn't so bad now. I can mange without help." The best time to create a team who helps is now. When you'll need more help, you'll have it.

5. Rely on help from community organizations.
Meals on Wheels, home care agencies and day care centers, to name just a few, may offer services that your caree needs.

   Contact your local Area Agency on Aging for a listing of services and organizations in your community. Visit your local medical equipment supply store to find devices and gadgets that enhance your caree's abilities and independence from you. Remember, allowing the help of others is a sign of strength.

   In addition, ask about local, state or federal programs (like the Veterans Administration's Aid and Attendant Care Program) that might provide financial assistance for you and/or your caree. As your caree's care needs increase, so will the costs associated with his or her care. Understanding what programs can help, in addition to understanding what your caree can afford, will help you plan appropriately for the future.

6. Keep your caree's wishes in mind.
When appropriate, ask for his or her input and ideas. How does your caree feel about living at home? What does your caree fear or dread? (These are also good questions to ask yourself, too.)

You may disagree with your caree's lifestyle choices. You may be incredibly exasperated by your caree's inability to accept help or make good decisions. Vent your frustations in your journal and to your support group. It's your caree's life, which means you want to respect his or her decisions.

If your caree suffers from a cognitive impairment, you'll want to step in and ensure your caree's safety. If you struggle to keep your caree safe, consider hiring an Aging Life Care Expert. (Visit www.aginglifecare.org for details.) You also can hire a Certified Caregiving Consultant (CCC), many of whom have already been through a caregiving experience, who can offer ideas, suggestions and solutions. (You can learn more about hiring a CCC at CareGiving.com.)

A Stumble: Because you are informed about community services and options, you may overlook your caree's ideas and suggestions.

A Steady: Your caree may be able to provide valuable insights and ideas about the services being provided. Be sure to include your caree, when appropriate, in any discussion regarding the care plan.

7. Reflect the changes in your journal.
How do you feel now? What are your concerns? Fears? What outcomes are you working toward? What losses have you noticed during this period? What changes in the relationship cause you to feel sad? What changes have given you comfort?

8. Start a second journal that you use to detail your caree's needs and your caregiving responsibilities.
Note any changes in your caree's health and condition so that you can confidently discuss your concerns during physician appointments. Take the journal with you to every doctor's appointment; jot down your questions to ask during doctor's appointments as well as take notes during the appointment. Use your journal as a caregiving manual, which will help when others step in to provide care. Continue to chronicle your caregiving journey in your first journal. What causes you to mourn?

9. Detail your caree's medical history, medications, hospitalizations, treatments and changes in medical status.
A searchable document, like a spreadsheet or an app like Evernote, will be handy throughout your caregiving experience. You'll be able to easily find details relating to important information, such as previous hospitalizations, medication changes and lab results.

10. Create the habit of regularly holding family meetings.
Judy, for instance, can meet with her adult children regularly to provide updates. Andy, whose family is uninvolved, can plan regular meetings with those who help Abigail. If you and your caree share a household with other family members (including children), consider creating House Rules.

Rules for the household may include:
- Who does what, how and when;
- Guidelines for fights, fun, and festivals (celebrations);
- Schedule of meetings and their purposes;
- Expectations in regard to support, engagement and participation.

If family members conveniently become unavailable for meetings, then send regular email updates. When you keep your family members informed of your caree's situation, you ensure your own peace of mind. Family members may choose to stay uninvolved but they have to live with that choice.

11. Manage the money. Develop a budget, keep track of expenses, set up a filing system for bills and receipts.
Keep your caree's expenses separate from yours and your family's. Keep track (and receipts) of any of your caree's bills that you pay. If you're overwhelmed, consider having a professional, like a financial planner or bank trust officer, oversee your caree's financial situation. You can hire a daily money manager to oversee the budget and pay the bills. (Visit https://secure.aadmm.com to find a money manager.)

12. Start a Solutions Fund so you can hire solutions.
The account funds solutions for boredom, breaks and back-up plans. Contribute a monthly amount; allow yourself flexibility in how you use the monthly budget. Use the fund for your caree, for the house, for you.

Use the Solutions Fund for your caree to hire services such as home health, adult day or to purchase games or products to keep your caree engaged.

Use the fund for your house (or your caree's) to hire a cleaning service, lawn maintenance, snow removal. The fund buys you services from a counselor or life coach or Certified Caregiving Consultant, or for pampering services, adult education classes and activities.

Ask family members to contribute to your Solutions Fund.

13. Have back-up plans and then back-up plans for your back-up plan. Ask yourself, "What if..." and then create a plan to manage the "What if's." Contact your local fire department (or your caree's fire department, if you live in different communities) to learn about emergency preparedness. If it can happen, most likely it will. Be ready with a plan. An Aging Life Care Expert or a Certified Caregiving Consultant can be invaluable in developing your back-up plans.

14. Help yourself, especially if your caree refuses help.
You may find great resources to help your caree, only to be shut down by a stubborn caree. As you spend more time with your caree, you'll have less time to keep up with your responsibilities. Hire out services to help you, like housecleaning and lawn maintenance, as often as you can. Even if you can only afford a housecleaning service once a year, do it. Do it when it will help you most.

In addition, keep up-to-date on community resources and providers. Although your caree may refuse help now, a day may come when you'll need to step in with help.

15. Let go of expectations, says Christopher-Charles Chaney, a Certified Caregiving Consultant and Educator. You may expect the health care system, your house of worship and your friends to step up and step in to help. They may. They may not. When they can't, work to find those who can.

16. Build your own paradise of privacy.
Call a spare bedroom or a corner in the basement your own. Add your favorite things (books, chocolate, candles, scrapbook, journal, music, TV, videos, photography, family photos) to make the space a retreat you love to use.

17. You are, and will continue to be, your caree's most important health care provider.

You have critical knowledge of your caree's health. More than anyone, you know your caree best, which means you are your caree's best advocate. Make sure you can receive regular updates about your caree by completing the necessary paperwork, like forms required through the Health Insurance Portability and Accountability Act (HIPAA), with your caree's providers.

18. Continue to maintain your healthy lifestyle.

Take note when the stress causes too much comfort food or too few walks. One of your best defenses against the impact of stress is a healthy lifestyle.

19. An apple a day…

What's your apple in this stage? What helps you to feel good on a daily basis?

Two Quick Tips:

1. You may find yourself "taking away" from your caree--the keys to the car, the solo trip to the grocery store, her hosting the large family get-togethers. **To balance the scales, try to replace what you take away.** The exchange may not be equal (and in most situations, it won't be), but giving back some of what you take away will help your caree maintain her dignity and independence.

For instance, you feel that it's just too much for your mother to continue hosting Thanksgiving dinner every year. Your mother reluctantly relents to having the celebration at your house. As you plan for the day, try to incorporate some of your mother's traditions in the celebration: her favorite recipes, her special dishes, her most honored prayer. While your mother may miss hosting the tradition at her home, she'll feel that some of her house is at yours.

2. **Have two bags packed (one for you and one for your caree) with toiletries and change of clothes ready in case your caree is suddenly hospitalized.** Your caree will have his or her comforts and necessities and you'll be able to settle in to your caree's hospital room to ensure proper care.

Some suggested items to pack in your hospital bag:

> –Pair of pajamas
>
> –Change of clothes, including a few pairs of underwear
>
> –A water bottle and healthy snacks
>
> –Toothbrush, toothpaste and other personal care items
>
> –Your medications
>
> –Phone numbers of family members and friends
>
> –A copy of your caree's durable power of attorney for health care and finances
>
> –Contact information for your caree's physician(s)
>
> –List of prior hospitalizations, surgeries, and medical conditions (along with dates)
>
> –Insurance cards

–A list of your caree's current medications and allergies

–A favorite book or magazine

–A book which brings you comfort and reminds you that you are okay

–A charger for your phone

–Notepad and pen so you can take notes when doctors and other health care professionals make visits.

The Freshman Caregiver
Your Reflections

In this stage, what are your goals?
—For your caree?

—For you and your family?

How will you achieve these goals?

Who can help you achieve these goals?

What are your struggles?
—In caring for your caree?

—In caring for you and your family?

How can you overcome these struggles?

The Freshman Caregiver
Your Resource Library

UGH! A Diagnosis. Now, What?

Life seems to stop after you hear a family member's diagnosis of an illness like cancer or Alzheimer's. But, life goes on. So how do you?

We've got tips to help manage the difficult few days after learning of a family member's medical diagnosis:

1. Believe the diagnosis gives you time. You have time to research, plan, communicate. You have time to get a second opinion; you have time to research the disease, its progression and treatment options. You have time to talk with your family member who has been diagnosed, with other family members and friends. You have time to make the most of the time you have.

2. Know denial about the diagnosis will steal your time. You may be tempted to disbelieve a diagnosis, to hide it. Denial, not the diagnosis, is the true enemy. In denial, you deny yourself the chance to learn, prepare, plan and understand. The progression of a disease will arrive on time; denial will make you late for its arrival. Playing catch-up after its arrival will waste precious time. And, before you know it, there won't be enough time. Don't let denial take your time.

3. Consider how well you and your family member respect and like your family member's health care professionals. The right physician and care team can make a huge difference. If you feel a disconnect during the discussion about the diagnosis, consider getting another opinion and finding another physician.

4. Talk about the diagnosis with your family member (if appropriate). Then, let your family member talk about the diagnosis with his or her own support system. Do the same for yourself; call a friend or a family member to talk about how it feels. And, talking about it with someone will help keep you from denial.

5. When you talk about the diagnosis with your family member, talk about your priorities. What's a priority for your family member? The most aggressive treatment? The best quality of life? Time with family? Time traveling? How do these priorities align with yours? How can you make the priorities a reality?

6. Let the news sink in. You've had a shock, no matter how expected the diagnosis. The news is shocking. You will feel different. Allow yourself to get used to your new skin, so to speak.

7. Start a journal to document how you feel and what this feels like. Even if you think you won't like journaling, you will like going to a place (your journal) where you get to let it all out. When it comes out, it somehow sorts itself out.

8. Contact organizations, like disease-specific agencies, that can provide information. Gather information and look for online communities that can provide help and support.

9. Take deep breaths. Sounds so simple but when news takes the wind out of you, breathing seems to be the last thing we remember to do. Take deep breaths.

10. Get out of the house. Take a walk, pick up take-out for dinner, stop at a friend's, go to the library. A change of scenery and the motion it takes to get there will help.

The FAQs of Caregiving

You're worrying that a family member or friend may need help in the near future. Or, you're starting to help a family member, which means you're starting to ask a lot of questions. To help, I've compiled the most frequently asked questions about caregiving and the answers you need.

1. Am I up to this? And, what if I'm not?
Everyone has his or her limits as a family caregiver. It's important to respect yours. It's impossible to do it all so look to the community, family, friends, health care professionals and volunteers to fill in the voids.

2. How much will this cost?
A large misconception exists that the government, through Medicare and/or Medicaid, will pay for care for your caree. Medicare, the federal insurance program typically for person's 65 and over, has very limited benefits to cover long-term care needs, either in a home or in a nursing home. Medicaid, a state-funded program typically for low-income persons, pays for the costs of in-home and nursing home care only when a caree's income is low enough to qualify for benefits.

The majority of costs associated with a chronic illness or disability are assumed by the family and/or the caree and/or private insurance (including long-term care insurance).

According to Genworth Cost of Care Survey, the monthly cost for caregiving services in 2017 are:
- Home health aide (provides dressing and bathing assistance): $4,000 per month
- Adult day service (provides socialization and meals): $1,500 per month
- Assisted living facility (base rate): $3,700 per month
- Nursing home (semi-private room): $7,150 per month

A financial planner can help you explore ways to finance care. You'll also want to get a durable power of attorney for health care and finances for your caree; an elder law attorney can help execute this important document.

3. How long can I expect to do this?

In our most recent survey of family caregivers, 48% of respondents have been caring for a family member for five years or more. When asked how much longer caregiving will last, 28% of respondents estimate that their experience will last another two to five years while 26% believe it will last another 10 years.

Because this is a long-term commitment, planning for the future is key. Take into account your caree's financial resources, your emotional resources and the community's resources. All these connect to make caregiving doable.

4. Who can I contact for help?

The ElderCare Locator which can refer you to your local Area Agency on Aging. Call 1-800-677-1116. You also can search for help at the BenefitsCheckup website: www.benefitscheckup.org.

5. How do I know when my family member can no longer live safely at home?

Spend time with your family member to learn the daily and weekly routines. Put systems into place which help to avoid a crisis. Personal emergency response systems, adult day services, home health aides, telephone check-in services, Meals on Wheels, and volunteer programs all help keep your caree safe.

In addition, AARP has checklists available to help you make changes in your caree's living environment. Visit aarp.org for details.

Often, a caree will resist changes. Usually what's behind the resistance is fear. Respect and recognize that these changes will be difficult for your caree. Start slowly, involve your caree, when appropriate, in any discussions and decisions. Ask for your caree's commitment to try any services for a month. Allow your caree to vent, without judgments or recriminations.

Reassure your caree that these services will keep him or her at home, safely, and that you want to work together to achieve this goal.

If your caree still refuses, then back off, at least for the time being.

However, don't give up. Contact local organizations (such as home health agencies, Meals on Wheels, assisted living facilities, rehab centers) for information about their services, costs and availability. In case a crisis occurs, you'll have the information you need to make good decisions about your caree's future.

6. Can I get paid to do this?

In some cases, you may be able to be paid for receiving care. You can check with your local Area Agency on Aging to find out if any problems in your community will reimburse you for the care you provide. Your caree's long-term care insurance policy may include a benefit that allows you to receive payment. You also can ask other family members or your caree to pay you. If you receive payment from your caree or other family members, you'll want to have a contract outlining your responsibilities and payments. Visit www.caregiver.org/personal-care-agreements for more information.

7. This is so depressing! I didn't realize I would feel this way. What can I do?

Often, family caregivers overlook an important part of their experience: The grief they feel at the losses suffered by the caree, by the family and by themselves.

It is depressing, which is why taking regular breaks is important. It's also critical to maintain some hobbies and interests you enjoy. Rejuvenating yourself on a regular basis will help you manage the experience.

In addition, finding support will help you unburden yourself, which will lighten your load. You can join an online support group and/or a group in your community.

8. How can I get help from other family members?

Often, family caregivers feel abandoned by family members, usually siblings, the very people they expected to help. So, how do you get your five brothers and sisters to help out?

Recognize that people are caregivers in different ways. Your brother the CPA breaks out into a rash at the idea of visiting your mother in the nursing home. Suggest that he call her every Sunday afternoon or write letters. Or, ask him to manage her financial affairs. Your sister is conveniently busy every time you ask her to spell you so you can take a break. Suggest that your sister help offset the costs of the companion sitter or home health aide you hire.

Should you force them to help? No. Be specific in your requests, but never demand that help be given. If your siblings refuse your requests for help, accept it. But, don't accept the idea that you are alone. Look to the community for help and for support.

You may find that the caregiving experience changes you and your relationships–another good reason to find support and camaraderie among those who will understand.

9. I feel so guilty–about everything.
Your caree will make you feel guilty. Which makes it only worse, as you already carry around enough guilt. How do you keep it at bay?

Keep your perspective. Consider, whose problem is this? Does your caree expect you to make him or her happy? That's not your job. Does your spouse badger you about the time you spend with your caree? Try to work out a compromise, so that you have a workable schedule for your spouse, your caree and yourself. Remember, you can only control yourself, your reactions, your words and your feelings. The rest is up to everyone else.

Asking for and receiving help also can help minimize your guilt. The wider you cast your net, the more help you receive, the better your caregiving experience will be for you and your caree. With more help, you'll open up the world, which caregiving will make smaller, to yourself and to your caree.

The Five Myths of Caregiving

You'll have ideas and thoughts about caregiving that would logically seem to be true. These ideas and thoughts seem like truths. Unfortunately, they are really myths.

Here are five myths about caregiving:

1. "My mom raised five children with little help. Surely, I can care for her on my own."
Caring for a frail older adult with chronic illness is not even in the same ballpark as raising children. Sure, you'll find similarities but the toll of caregiving on your emotions will wear down even the most resolute. Caregiving can be depressing, lonely, overwhelming. Parenting has challenging moments, but it's an experience that can light up your world. Sometimes, you'll feel like caregiving has darkened it. And, that's why it's good to find help and support.

2. Everyone you helped in the past will gladly pitch in to help now.
Move in your elderly grandfather with dementia and watch your close circle of friends scatter. Tell them you're feeling stressed and witness eye-rolls and impatient sighs. "Why not just put him in a nursing home?," they'll advise. Ask for help—hey, haven't you always been there to pitch in?—and you'll be asking to an empty room. Not everyone disappears, but the number of those who do can be heartbreaking.

3. Your caregiving situation is so strange and bizarre you'll never find anyone who can help or understand.
A husband who urinates in the planter. A grandmother who swears like a sailor. A mother who believes a clean house is one cleaned 20 years ago. You may think you've got a caregiving situation to take the cake and that there is absolutely, positively no help. Try. Professionals who work in social services agencies and eldercare agencies will not bat an eye when you share your story. If they do, find another staff member or agency. It's embarrassing to you, but to a professional, it's just part of their day.

4. Conversely: All your friends and family members will understand exactly how you feel.
You can look at your caree and feel like you can read his heart and mind. So, depending on what you read, you react. You take care. Because you

can, you think others can, too. Sigh. Many can't. It would be wonderful if they could, but they can't. It's not a poor reflection on them or on you—it's just a fact. Because they can't, you can. Tell them what you need and how you feel. You'll both feel better for it.

5. It's easy to find the treatment and care your caree needs.
With a good doctor, it can be a fairly smooth ride (bumps to be expected) to an appropriate diagnosis, treatment and care plan. But with a bad doctor, it can be a nightmare. Trust your gut, advocate for your caree and demand answers. Often, you are working against the clock, so move quickly if you feel your caree (and you) need better and different physicians and professionals. A support group can be particularly helpful; members can suggest alternatives and options that work for them.

Your Caregiving Mission Statement

Fate may have brought you to this place, this caregiving role. Fate through a car accident, a sudden stroke or just your caree's age-related frailties.

Fate may have waved her hand and tapped you to be the family caregiver. You can add some controls to your caregiving destiny with your own caregiving mission statement.

Your mission statement reflects your caregiving goals and your caregiving personality. Your mission statement will serve as a reminder of what you can and cannot do as a family caregiver as well as what's most important to you and to your caree.

In your mission statement, consider including the following:

Your respite schedule
For instance, your respite schedule may include breaks on Wednesday evenings, Sunday afternoons, one weekend every three months, two weeks annually. You'll know best how often you need breaks in order to stay on purpose with a healthy perspective.

Your respite service plan
In order to take regular breaks, you'll use myriad help in various combinations. Help can come from a schedule that combines help from community programs, service providers and family members and friends.

Your ongoing care goals
Your mission statement also reflects your stragegy for managing when your caree's needs increase.

Your dreams for yourself
What's important to you? Which values drive your decisions? Which choices can you keep in your day?

Your hopes as a family caregiver
How do you measure success during a life that includes caregiving responsibilities? How can you redefine success? How can you achieve success?

Your wishes for your caree

You'll want to include your thoughts about quality medical care and dignified interactions with health care professionals.

Your caree's wishes

A helpful mission statement also includes your caree's definition of quality of life, thoughts on receiving help and care, wishes about end-of-life and desires on how to spend his or her last years, months and days. If your caree is unable to communicate these wishes to you, your knowledge of his or her past lifestyle and relationships will help you determine these issues.

Your mission statement is a work in progress. As you change, as your caree changes, as community services change, as your own immediate family changes, so shall your mission statement. Keep each version of your mission statement in your caregiving journal as you'll find helpful perspectives when you review and revisit each one.

Forming Your Caregiving Team

The lie about caregiving is that you have to go it alone. It's a powerful lie because it seems like you must go it alone because it looks like you're the only one who does.

The truth is that caregiving is too big and too demanding for one person. You deserve a team to help. If you think about it, you already have some team members. It's just that you just haven't seen them as such. For instance, on a bad day, maybe your dog, Trixie, provides the love and healing you need. Well, guess what, Trixie is on your team. Maybe your trips to the drugstore are helpful because of that nice pharmacist, Bruce, who always has a smile and a helpful tip to share. Yep, Bruce has made the team.

The first step to forming your team is to determine why you need a team. So, write your answers to this question: Why do I need a team?

Your answers may be:
- For support
- For answers
- For breaks
- For laughs
- For reassurance
- For errand-running
- For bill-paying
- For hands-on care
- And on and on.

Next, answer this question: What responsibilities do I want to delegate to my team?

Your answers may be:
- Provide a three-hour break twice a week
- Provide a one-week break every year
- Research community options for me
- Lend an objective ear
- Keep me realistic in my role.

Once you understand the purpose and role of your team, you're ready to build it. Again, you may already have some members; some you may have to recruit. Some family members and friends will run when you appear clipboard in hand, ready to recruit. That's okay—they are not the team members you need.

Next, answer: Who do I want on my team?

Your answers may be:

- The caregiver specialist at the Area Agency on Aging
- The home health aide
- The librarian
- My best friend
- My support group
- My neighbor
- My local assisted living facility
- My brother.

Here's an example of how we can put it all together:

I'm a full-time caregiver to my mom. I manage well except on Saturday afternoons when I feel cooped up. I find that I hate staying home with my mom on Saturday afternoons. I also want help with cooking because my cooking is awful. I wish I could find more time to read a book each week. I also have lots of anger about my situation and want someone to vent to.

With this in mind, I decide I want a team to help me get out a few Saturdays each month, relieve me of some of cooking responsibilities, free up some time for me to read more and provide an objective ear.

I decide that my team can include a home health aide to stay with my mom, a family member to prepare frozen meals that I can microwave, the librarian to update me when a good book arrives and a support group member to be my venting buddy.

I'm ready to start recruiting!

Home health aide
I call local agencies to find an agency that can best meet my needs. I

interview home health aides and work with the agency to find the right professional caregiver for myself and my caree. And, what the heck, I ask my brother to foot the bill. I call him and say, "I'd love your help with Mom. I'd like to take three hours off two Saturdays a month. I found a great aide to stay with Mom while I'm gone. Can you help out with the expense--it would mean so much to me."

Frozen meals

I send my family members and friends an update e-mail. I let them know how much it means to be able to take care of our caree and how grateful I am for their support. I am running into one problem, though, I write. I'm a terrible cook! I'd love some help. Would you be able to help with a few frozen meals each week that I can microwave?

Books

I call my local library and explain my situation to the librarian. I miss reading great books, I explain, but my time constraints make getting to the library difficult. In addition, I'm completely out of ideas as to which books are worth reading. Can you help?

Venting Buddy

I ask a member of my support group if he or she would be interested in being venting partners. We'll call each other every week, I suggest. I vent for 10 minutes while my support group friend merely listens. Then, it's his turn.

As with all things, the recruiting process may have starts-and-stops, which is okay. Keep asking until you find the right solution.

And, for those team members you didn't have to recruit (like Trixie and Bruce) be sure to include them in your regular thanks to the team. Your gratitude and appreciation keeps your team full.

The Power of Requesting Right

Can we get the help we want? Beth Ruske, a managing partner at Tiara Coaching (www.tiaracoaching.com), assures us we can. She shares ways to make clear and powerful requests for help.

Here's how:

1. **Recognize it is our own responsibility to know what we need or what would be helpful.** Spend some time asking yourself what kind of help you need or want. Is it financial, is it time away from your caree? Is it sharing the burden or caregiving responsibilities? Get clear about what would be helpful for you.

2. **Be willing to make specific requests.** We think others can read our minds and anticipate our needs. They can't.

3. **Make the request and then allow the other person the freedom of three responses:**
   - Yes. If they say "yes," thank them and expect them to fulfill the request.
   - No. "No" is a little more challenging. Remember the person is NOT saying no to you. They are saying no to the request you made. Beth's standard reply is, "Thanks for saying no. I'd like to ask why? Is there a perspective that would be useful for me?"
   - Renegotiate. Renegotiating is a wonderful reply. The person is willing and engaging with you, telling you exactly what would work for them. Now you get to answer their renegotiation with your own "yes", "no", or counter-renegotiation. It's about give and take.

Remember that if you are attached to a "yes" from someone, then you're making a demand, rather than a request. Others have to have the freedom to say "no."

Beth also shared tips when you're working with service providers, like home health agencies.
   - If we know what would be helpful, then ask straight out. If we don't know what help we need, then explain the situation and ask,

"What special help do you think you could provide that would help this situation?"

- Be open to a win-win solution. Often times, that means compromises and negotiation. Be open to the idea of looking at solutions in a different way.
- Relieve yourself from having to make the "right decision." If you can gather the information from trusted resources, then let it sit and know you will make the best choice you can. Your instincts are still the best guide you have. No one can tell you what to do—that will come from you.
- If you come from a win-win perspective and you are willing to make the best choice you can at any given moment, you are doing the best you can, which is all that you can do: Your best in any given moment. Your best today doesn't mean the same thing as your best tomorrow. Just commit to giving your best in any given moment.

Finally, don't expect perfection from yourself or others. Again, just strive to provide your best in any given moment. In those moments, have compassion with yourself and others.

7 Traits of a Hope-full Family Caregiver

In *The Seven Desires of Every Heart* by Mark Laaser and Debra Laaser, the authors tell us what every heart wants: to be heard, affirmed, blessed, safe, touched, chosen. This book's title reminded me of Stephen Covey's book, *The Seven Habits of Highly Effective People, Powerful Lessons in Personal Change*.

Which brings me to consider family caregivers. What characteristics or traits are important to have in a caregiving role? I created the seven traits but then stumbled. What do these traits lead to? Empowerment? Health? Then it hit me: Hope. Caregiving seems bereft of hope. These traits, I think, can help bring it back.

Resilient Backbone

It's a war out there. Or, rather in there--the bedroom, the bathroom, the car. And, then when you leave the house, it's a war in the doctor's office, the hospital, your sibling's house. Or, so it seems.

Battles become part of the experience: The battle of the wills with your caree; the battle to find and receive the care you want for your caree; the battle to find and receive the help you want; the battle with yourself to stay patient, positive, to persevere. You'll get battle-weary, but a rebounding backbone is the best ammunition. Your resilient backbone means you keep an objective viewpoint (it's often not about you, but them), a belief in yourself and your abilities, a faith that props and comforts you, and a reliance on your best asset—your gut.

Flexible Goals

When you begin your caregiving experience, your goal may be to keep your caree home until the end. Then, the disease progresses, the house becomes an obstacle, the help disappears. Your goal may change to finding the best possible place to provide the care your caree needs.

It's okay when your goals change. Very little about the caregiving experience stays the same. Your goals should be as fluid as the experience, refining and updating as you go. Your Caregiving Mission Statement can help you set and revise your goals.

Escape Routes

Maybe it's not Route 66, but your escape route takes you to the place where you can vent, scream and cry. The highway may lead to be your support group, your best friend, your pet.

Your road also may wind to the sanctuary you create in your house. Your sanctuary may be a corner of your bedroom, complete with your favorite photos, music, books and flowers. Your sanctuary may be that monthly golf game with your friends. Or, it could just be five minutes alone in your kitchen, when you can sit at the table with your eyes closed and day dream.

Plan your escape routes and put them into practice.

Bulldog Tenacity

Caregiving can be a bulldozer. To avoid tire marks on your forehead, be tenacious in a bulldog way. Know that your efforts will bring you answers, help and support. Accept no less.

Loud Laughter

Caregiving strips you naked, leaving you raw. That's good. Now you know what's important. Your loudest laugh, demonstrating how much you appreciate the joy and blessings in life, proves that. You can laugh because, amazingly, you've discovered life's secret: the moments, those 30-seconds of shared smiles of knowing, of close contact of love, of the combined power of compassion, matter most.

Resourceful Network

You're only one person which is why you tap into a network of resources. Be truthful with yourself about what you need. Then, build a team to get it.

Forgiveness and Then Some

Oh, so many to forgive—family members, friends, your caree, the disease and its relentless progression, your community, your faith, yourself. Does your heart and soul have enough to go around?

Yes, because living in unforgiveness only hurts you—no one else, not even those you may perceive to be unworthy of your forgiveness. The persons most difficult to forgive are those who act, and react, from fear. Resenting the fear-ful in your life weighs you down with their fears; forgiving them frees you. Although it can sometimes seem otherwise, people are doing their best. Believe that and move on to find the best possible for you and your situation.

So, you ask, where's the hope? The hope in caregiving lies in knowing that the cure for life is to live it, regardless of severity of struggles. Living fully, even around and within the struggles, opens you to unimagined blessings.

Should Dad Move In?

Karen and her husband thought they had the answer. Her father was living alone. They worried about him. They found it difficult to be at his house to help him and be at their home to provide for their two children. So, her father moved in with them.

A year later, Karen finally feels the family is adjusting to the living arrangement. "It was so much harder than I ever thought it would be," Karen says. Karen had a difficult time understanding how to help her father, who sat day after day in front of the television. Her suggestions to join the local senior center or a men's club were met with a "No, thanks." Much to her surprise, Karen often found herself feeling frustrated, helpless, and even resentful.

Moving your caree to your home does make caregiving more convenient. But, it also significantly changes the make-up of your household. Questions to keep in mind as you consider such a move:

1. How will your house make room for everyone? Will a family member be "uprooted" from a bedroom in order to make room for your caree?

2. How will each family member have some privacy, either their own room or their own space within a room? If everyone has their own space, everyone can get a break. And, on a regular basis, everyone will need a break from each other.

3. How will your house adjust to your caree's care needs? With increasing care needs comes the need for handicap accessible rooms. Is your home disability friendly?

4. How do you and other family members, especially your spouse, enjoy the relationship with your caree? Living under one roof intensifies the relationship. If you don't get along when you don't live together, chances are you really won't get along when you live together. If that's the case, is it best to house the relationship under one roof?

5. How will your caree receive the socialization that he needs?
In order to make the decision that's right for your family, research all options in your community: retirement communities, assisted living facilities, home health care, adult day centers.

You may find that your caree can remain in her home with home care and by attending an adult day center. Or, you may find that an assisted living facility offers the help and activities that he needs and enjoys. Or, you may find that your home is just the right place.

Caregiving or Your Career?

You're facing a big decision—should you quit your job in order to focus solely on your caregiving responsibilities? Such a decision comes after researching and exploring options. Here are some areas to consider:

1. The budget needed to provide care at home in your absence. Will you better meet the budget if you work and hire in-home care? Or, quit your job to stay home and provide the care yourself? Your budget should also include regular breaks for you. If you stay home, budget an amount to spend on services weekly so you can take a break. If you continue to work, still budget an amount for regular breaks, whatever you feel you will need. And, whether you continue to work or choose to stay home, budget an amount that provides for regular breaks for you from caregiving.

2. Community services. Are you taking advantage of all of the services available to your relative? Visit this site to see what services your caree is eligible to receive: www.benefitscheckup.org. How would availability of services, services you were not aware of, impact your decision?

3. Your caregiving personality. Will you manage okay at home, without heading out to the office every day? Do you enjoy the break from caregiving that your job provides? Or, will you be miserable at work worrying about your mom? Or, would a part-time job that allows you to get regular breaks from caregiving while pursuing a career and earning income work best for you?

4. Your future. How will a loss of income affect your future? How will you keep up-to-date on trends that impact your industry and the workplace? If you know you'll need to return to work, how will you ensure your skills remain relevant?

5. Input of other family members, friends, support group members. What are their concerns for you? What suggestions, insights can they offer?

6. The length of time your caree may need your help. Can you afford to stay home for two years? Five years? As long as your caree needs you? In our most recent survey of family caregivers, 44% say that they estimate their caregiving experience will last another five years. Would you be able to manage that long without a salary? With a full-time job?

As you know, chronic illness and disability can be deceiving; longevity often cannot be predicted. And, there's no better cure than loving care from a family member. If you stay at home, be sure you understand how long you can manage without a salary. And, start making plans now for when that time comes when you need a salary. Which assisted living facilities are good in your community? Which nursing homes provide the best care? Which home health agencies have staff qualified to care for your caree?

7. Your human resource department. Does your company offer flex time? Sabbaticals? Work from home? Job sharing? Family Medical Leave Act? What options does your employer offer? Would these options make caregiving and working easier?

8. Your current needs. Do you need a short period of time off from work, to find services, to hire in-home caregivers, to remodel your home? Would taking such a leave make it possible for you to accommodate your caree's care needs so that you can return to work full-time? Sometimes, we tend to view solutions as being all or nothing, but the best solution may exist somewhere in between.

9. Assistance of other family members and friends. Would other relatives be willing to share the care, commit to a schedule of caregiving? (I know you're shaking your head "No", but why not ask? If they say no, you're in no worse shape than before you asked.)

10. Your own health. If you quit your job, what provisions will you make for your own medical insurance? Will you have the insurance coverage necessary to ensure you stay healthy?

11. Your peace of mind. Compromises are always involved, whether you stay at home, take a part-time job, or work a full-time job. Which compromises can you live with?

Lasting Caregiving: Embrace Your Limits

Limits are our reality check; they are the facts that relate to our self-control. We have the idea that we have a limited amount of self-control. Not so. Self-control is a limited resource, which must be protected. When you have control, we behave as we want. When we are out-of-control, well... We behave in a way that brings remorse, shame and guilt. Limits protect our self-control.

Limits also take care of your ability to give care. Limits are just like your body getting tired at the end of the day. Limits let you know when you need a break, a change, a difference.

Lasting caregiving very much depends on understanding and embracing your limits.

Understand your limits as they relate to:
- Time: Our day imposes a natural limit.
- Space: Everyone (including caregiving) needs their own space.
- Money: There's only so much; how can you use it well?
- Stomach: Caregiving is not for the faint of heart or stomach.
- Strength: Sometimes, it's physically demanding. It's always emotionally draining.
- Disease Process: Your caree will decline. While it feels unnatural, it's the natural part of life.
- Resources: Depending on where you live and how much money your caree has, you may have a lot or some or minimal resources.
- Energy: We think we can go on and on and on. Our body, though, will tell us otherwise.
- Heart: Your values and priorities guide your decisions.

Consider your limits as they relate to:

Time
What's your limit in how much time you spend with your caree? What's your limit in spending time with family who can't support you? What's your limit in when and how much you talk about caregiving (i.e., updates to others)?

Space

What's your limit in how much space you share? What's your limit in how much space caregiving takes?

Money

How much is available to spend on care? How much is needed? What options are available?

Stomach

What can't you stomach? When you can't, who can?

Disease Process

If the disease-process becomes bigger than you, your team and the house, who and what can take over?

    Once in awhile
    During the day
    During the night
    During the role

Your Strength

What's your physical limit during the day and week? During your role? What's your emotional limit during the day and week? During your role?

Your Resources

What community organizations can help? Which organizations support you? When are you most resourceful? When do you need to be resourceful?

Your Heart

How does your life today line up with your priorities? What do you live your values?

When we set limits, we live life on our terms. We live the life we want, not the life others think we "should." With limits, you give care your way.

Tip for a Tough Day: Appoint a Love Substitute

As you work to stay healthy in your caregiving role, consider the five traits of well-being, as described in Positive Psychology: Hope, Gratitude, Zest, Curiosity and Giving and Receiving Love.

The first four traits of well-being build from our capacity to love and be loved. When we accept love (and help) from others, we allow them to fulfill one of their basic needs (to love).

In caregiving, you may feel you are the only one who gives to your caree. And, you will have days when giving love to your caree just seems like an impossible task. When you can't, you feel incredibly guilty or awfully resentful. UGH!

Instead of feeling guilty or resentful, appoint a love substitute.

A love substitute can be a letter written to your caree from someone your caree loves. You can ask family members to regularly write letters to your caree. During those tough moments, when your caree needs love and you need a break, share one of the letters. That's a love substitute.

Take advantage of the times you do feel the love by writing a letter to your caree that expresses that love; this letter becomes a love substitute. When you feel empty and your caree needs to feel full, you can share your letter. "Here's something I wrote the other day," you can say, "I'd love to read it to you."

Love substitutes also may be a pet, a phone call from a family member, a DVD of a family member's wedding, a comforting photograph or a favorite song. It's okay sometimes that it's not you. Stock up with a stable of love substitutes for your caree. Knowing your caree can receive love from several sources—not just you—can help you feel like you have room to breathe and time to feel that you also are loved.

"Either/Or" Can Become "And"

In caregiving, the world can seem to consist of "either...or." The world, then, might become these thoughts:

- Either I put my needs second or my caree doesn't have his needs met.
- Either I stay with my caree constantly or bad things will happen.
- Either I put my life on hold or my caree will not have what he needs when he needs it.

Thinking these statements is much different than reading them. When you think them, they may seem to make sense. Because you worry about your caree and because you understand your caree's complicated care needs, it's easy to understand why these thoughts seem to make sense.

But, when you speak them, they seem insane. With these thoughts, you put qualifiers on caregiving, that all hangs on you; you control the outcomes, the results. Oh, my, that's a heavy burden to bear. And, truly, how much of a disease process can you really control?

Not much.

Consider how you can move from "either...or" to "and." With "and" in the mix, your thoughts may be like this:

- I can take time for myself to pursue my own interests and my caree will be okay.
- I can make myself a priority and my caree's care needs will be met.
- I can set boundaries in my relationship with my caree and we both will better because of it.

These statements, when both thought and spoken, sound loving, kind and respectful—thoughts deserving of you. It is possible to have both—times when you become the priority and your caree still receives quality care.

When you get caught in the "either...or" mindset, how can you move toward adding "and"?

As Caregiving Rules, Rewrite the Rules

What rules you? Consider the following thoughts which may rule you:
- "My caree has more pressing needs than I, so my self-care must take a back seat to my caree's."
- "I'll take care of myself if I have the time."
- "I have too much to do to think about myself."

You can see how these rules can limit as well as harm. Consider creating new rules that reflect the importance of self-care, such as:
- "I provide the best care I can to my caree. During the day, I devote as much time as I can to activities and relationships important to me."
- "I balance caring for my caree with caring for myself."

More rules which may keep you less than you:
- "A good daughter would stay home in her mother's time of need."
- "You are responsible for my happiness."
- "So many depend on me—I must stay strong."
- "My caree is seriously ill; my attitude and behavior must reflect the serious nature of this situation."

You can re-write those rules with these:
- "I am a good daughter."
- "I am responsible for my own happiness and for decisions related to my happiness."
- "I stay strong by giving and receiving in equal amounts as much as possible."
- "I can see how precious life is, so now I'm the first to share a laugh and enjoy a good time."

These rules will change as you and your caree change. For instance, when your caree is terminal, you probably can't imagine spending time away from your caree. This priority (time together) becomes one of your caregiving values. You know that time may be limited so it's critical you spend the time you have together.

In this situation, a rule may be:

- "I take care of myself because I want to be in good health so I can enjoy every moment I have with my husband."

You hear this all the time: You must take care of yourself. It's true, but it's also true that how you take care of yourself must align with your current caregiving values. And, as your caregiving role changes, so will your caregiving values. For instance, when you first begin to help your caree, you may value the time you have away from your caree. In this case, your self-care rule may be:
- "I help my caree every evening. When I'm not helping my caree, I focus on my own relationships, needs and goals."

During an intense caregiving period (when your caree has the flu, for instance, or is recovering from a set-back), you may value the home health aide you've hired. Your rule may be:
- "Because of the pressure I feel in my caregiving role, I am taking breaks while the home health aide cares for my caree. My breaks are important to my endurance, so I will schedule the home health aide for three days a week for four hours at a time."

And, during those times when you feel trapped by caregiving, your self-care rule may be:
- "I have formed a team who can provide what my caree needs in order to be safe and cared for. Because of the team, I can take regular time away from my caregiving role. I cherish these breaks and know they are good for me and for my caree."

When your caree is experiencing heightened anxiety, your rule may be:
- "It's important for me to be available to my caree in order to relieve his anxiety. I will plan my breaks to write in my journal and listen to my favorite music when my caree naps and sleeps."

Your self-care rules work in tandem with your caregiving mission statement. And, your rules and your mission statement are yours to create. They are individualized just for you.

Take time to write your self-care rules, which reflect your current values.

Effective Family Meetings

Hold regular family meetings, which could be weekly or monthly or quarterly or when:

- Caregiving begins and one individual takes on the role of primary family caregiver
- Your caree experiences a change in condition, including a hospitalization
- You need more help
- You need a break
- You and other family members have differing opinions about a care plan or course of treatment
- End-of-life care care must be decided.

Your meetings can take place in person, over the phone or via video conference.

Create "Rules of Engagement" for your meetings; these rules hold everyone accountable for expected behaviors. The rules may be:

- Only one person speaks at a time
- Everyone has an opportunity to be heard
- An agenda, complete with time restraints, accompanies every meeting
- The agenda is limited to the Top 3, but no more than the Top 5, priorities
- Meetings end with consensus on action items
- Agree to disagree.

Let this question guide your discussions and decisions: What's best for our caree?

When your family is ready to make a decision, you can use a tool called Fist-to-Five Consensus Building to gauge support for or against the action or plan. It's a terrific, objective vehicle to express opinions while taking steps to resolve any outstanding concerns.

When making a decision or finalizing a plan, ask meeting participants to vote by showing a fist or a number of fingers that corresponds to their opinion.

Fist

A "No" vote, which will block consensus. A fist says "I need to talk more on the proposal and require changes for it to pass."

1 Finger

One fingers says, "I still need to discuss certain issues and suggest changes that should be made."

2 Fingers

"I am more comfortable with the proposal but would like to discuss some minor issues."

3 Fingers

"I'm not in total agreement but feel comfortable to let this decision or a proposal pass without further discussion."

4 Fingers

"I think it's a good idea/decision and will work for it."

5 Fingers

"It's a great idea and I will be one of the leaders in implementing it."

Anyone holding up fewer than three fingers should discuss their objections. The group then works to address these concerns. As you modify and adapt the plans and decisions, then continue to vote until you reach consensus (each individual votes with three fingers or higher) or you decide to move on to the next issue.

Source: Fletcher, A. (2002). *FireStarter Youth Power Curriculum: Participant Guidebook*. Olympia, WA: Freechild Project.

Sometimes, They Just Don't Help

We all hear (and I often say) that asking for help is imperative during a situation like caregiving. You simply have too much to do to do it all yourself.

This is completely true.

Sometimes, though, the message to ask for help doesn't represent the complete picture.

A few years ago, I attended a webinar during which the experts kept reiterating that family caregivers need to ask for help. For some reason, this really rubbed me the wrong way. The advice sounded hollow. I wondered if they really understood how complicated that simple advice can be.

Because I'm very interested in the experience of getting help during caregiving, I added a question about how often others help you in our annual survey. Consider the results from our 2017 survey (our latest):

How often do other family members help you?

They don't help	48.86%
Once a week	11.36%
Several times a month	10.23%
Once a month	10.23%
Three or more times a year	10.23%
Several times a week	9.09%

I asked the follow-up question, Why don't they help?

They live out-of-town	46.84%
I've asked, but they refuse	22.78%
I am the only one	18.99%
Other (write-in answers)	33.00%

Write-in answers to this question included:

They simply don't want the responsibility. They would prefer that he be in a nursing home.

I am retired and we have no children. The others have children and careers.

The family that lives here in town are busy with their own lives.

They do not offer. I would not accept if they did.

I'm the daughter. They EXPECT this from me.

Personal time, plan other activities before checking if assistance is needed, sometimes it's hard for them to accept what's happening.

They might help mom in an emergency, but not me.

They live in denial.

Too busy.

They are busy with their families or do not care.

Not emotionally capable.

They live out of town, but have not even visited. Don't seem interested in "being there" for us.

Their lives are too busy.

My daughter in college lives with us and helps, my sister helps when possible but her husband is in stage 4 cancer.

I really don't know or understand why they don't help. I do not want to bother by asking if I don't have to. I know they know its getting more challenging but they don't really offer.

They seem to think this is totally my responsibility.

I don't know. Scared, selfish or both.

They just don't want to be bothered.

I guess what bothered me most about the comments I heard during the webinar is that lack of recognition that it's hard to ask for help! It's hard to ask for help every week for a situation that can last ten years and longer. During a recent presentation I gave to a group of family caregivers, one family caregiver shared this insight: It's easy to help when you only have to help for a week or two. Finding someone who will help you for years is tough.

I often think of Michelle, a former family caregiver I met at a mutual friend's baby shower. She's one of five children. One brother helped her care for their parents. She asked and asked and asked and asked the other three siblings to help. They just didn't (or wouldn't).

I also was bothered by the idea that it's because the family caregiver doesn't ask for help that the experience is really difficult. Asking for help and then not receiving help makes the situation heart-breaking and really depressing. Sometimes, we're reticent to ask for help. At times, we don't ask because we feel it's important that we complete the task or responsibility. At times, we don't because it's hard to keep asking for help. At times, we don't simply because we don't have anyone to ask to help.

We all need help. It's true. It's just not as simple as asking for help when you're caring for a family member with a chronic illness or injury or frailty. And, it's never easy when you take into account the family dynamics and dysfunction.

The Help Arrived, But Left Too Early

You hear this all the time. If someone offers to help, accept it! So, you do.

A neighbor offers to help. He works in the home care industry and has volunteered to install those grab bars in the bathroom. You've been meaning to do this ever since your caree's arrival home from the hospital but there just never seems to be enough time, energy or money to get it done. So, your neighbor offers, tells he has what he needs to have the grab bars up on a Saturday. It won't be any problem, he assures you, he's happy to help.

Well, now it's the Thursday after the Saturday and the grab bars have been installed, well, sort of. They hang–dangle, really–in the bathtub, completely unusable. Your neighbor, it turns out, had never installed grab bars before. And, well, technically, he still hasn't. You finally call the hardware store and hire a staff member from the store to install the bars. It costs more than you want to spend. But, you need the bars. And, you need a usable bathroom. Now it's the following Saturday and you seem to be dangling: You can't seem to shake your anger.

Mostly, you're mad at yourself. You ask your caree, "How could I have let this happen?" Although it may seem that you've made a mistake, you haven't. You just didn't put safeguards in place. And, that's nothing more than a lesson learned.

The next time a kind offer arrives, some tips to keep in mind:

1. It's okay to ask about experience or skills when someone offers to complete a job that requires a certain amount of knowledge and talent. If it seems that the volunteer doesn't have what's needed to complete the job, then counter-offer: "I think this is a job for the Home Depot guy," you might say. "But, I'd love for you to go to Home Depot and help me hire the right guy."

2. While nitpicking isn't necessary, it is necessary to have a job completed so that it functions and makes your life easier. If it isn't and doesn't, communicate what you'd like done differently. If your requests aren't honored, ask if someone else could finish the work. If you can't get a

referral, look to other family members and friends for suggestions on who could complete the task.

3. Be gracious and grateful, even if the project wasn't completed correctly. Tell yourself: You're on your way to getting what you want.

4. Stay involved. It's okay to ask for updates, as the project moves forward, as well as to ask how you can help. Be calm and direct in your communication and ready to negotiate when necessary.

5. Expect the best, but prepare for the worst. Always have a Plan B, C and D–just in case. You never know.

6. Finally, believe in your ability to resolve challenges and obstacles as they arise. When the help doesn't help, you'll stumble from the impact. You'll steady when you face forward, take another step and decide you can find better help.

Your Contingency Plan

What if I'm sick? Who will take care of my caree?

What if I need to help my daughter and her new baby? Who will take care of my caree?

What if I need to go back to work? Who will take care of my caree?

These questions, which can seem to plague, actually are helpful--they propel you to create your contingency plan.

Here's how to create your plan:

Research is your first step. If you haven't called local social services agencies and services providers (including churches and synagogues) in more than one year, then start by checking with them. Funding changes, personnel changes, goals and missions change. An agency that couldn't help in the past now may have a program that will help you.

Remember: Your goal is to gather as much information as possible. If you learn about a program that you don't think your caree will like…wipe the thought from your head! Gather information about all programs--costs, availability, qualifications, contact person. The program may not be appropriate now, but may very well be the answer to your prayers down the road.

Next, check with family and friends. In an emergency, what kind of help can they offer? Who will be the second contact in case of an emergency?

Once you've researched all available options in the community and with your family and friends, then make a list. Include agency name, program name, program description, program details (cost, availability, etc.), agency phone number. You may also want to jot down appropriate times for these services to be used. For instance, short-term stays in nursing homes could be used when you need to take a week off.

During this process, you also can create your safety net, the net that catches when something falls. Consider:

Financial safety net

Who manages the finances? Who's the back-up? And, who is the check who makes sure finances are in good order?

Day-to-day caregiving

Who can back you up? Who can step in if you are sick? Your back-up can be family, friends, home health agencies, adult day services, assisted living facilities, nursing homes, Meals on Wheels, volunteer programs, personal emergency responses, phone check-in services, or a combination. Does your back-up have the necessary knowledge and training to back you up? And, what's your back-up for your back-up?

Losses

As your caree declines, how will you compensate for the losses? How will you manage when your caree can no longer drive and manage household responsibilities? What will need to change when caregiving needs intensify? Which services, family members, providers and other options can compensate?

You're out of commission

The flu, unexpected responsibilities, or a sore back makes caregiving that much more difficult. What gadgets and equipment can help until you feel better?

As a family caregiver, you know that the world can change without warning. You don't want to be caught off guard and without options. Your contingency plan and safety net ensure the well-being of you and your caree just in case "What if" really happens.

Your Bad Weather Back-Up

You watch the snow build from your office window. Or, you watch the storm clouds roll in--you know another doozy is on its way. You're supposed to stop at your mom's house on your way home from work. If you stop to help her, you wonder how you'll ever make it home. If you don't stop to help her…

When bad weather comes between you and your caree, consider these quick tips:

1. **Check with your caree's physician and specialists for suggestions** on how to ensure your caree is safe during weather emergencies.

2. If your caree receives care from a home health aide hired by a home care agency, **check with the agency's director to determine its protocol during snowstorms**. If an aide can't make it to work, will another be assigned? What other options are available?

3. If your caree relies on important regular treatments (dialysis, chemotherapy, wound care, oxygen delivery), **work with the service provider to create a safe back-up plan.**

4. If you've hired a home care worker privately, **be sure to create a back-up plan if the home care worker must cancel because of weather conditions**. (Use this back-up plan year-round and if your home care worker becomes ill, quits, or just doesn't work out.)

5. If you have family in the area and they regularly help, **create a "tag team" system that you can use during a weather emergency.** Determine which family member will stop at your caree's home, which family member is the back-up and how communication between the "tag team" will occur.

6. **Keep extra caregiving supplies** (incontinence supplies, over-the-counter medications, medications, canned goods, frozen meals) and extra boredom-fighting supplies (books, videos, puzzles, crossword puzzles, stationery) on hand at your caree's house and at your house, just in case.

7. **Create a space in your caree's house for your own personal supplies** (a change of clothes, toiletries, medications) that you may need in case you must spend the night.

8. **Use online services to order medications and food for delivery** to your caree's home.

9. **Check with your caree's town and county about assistance they offer to homebound and/or frail older adults during weather emergencies.** You can call the ElderCare Locator at 1-800-677-1116 for a referral to the Area Agency on Aging in your caree's community.

10. **Ask neighbors of your caree if they can pitch in by stopping to check on your caree.** Let them know how they can reach you in case of an emergency. Be sure someone you trust who lives near your caree's home has an extra set of keys.

11. **Hire teenagers in your caree's neighborhood to shovel.**

12. If your caree lives in a rural area or has a long walk to the mailbox, **check with the local post office to ensure that mail delivery occurs at your caree's front door.**

13. If you work, **check with your employer's Work/Life benefit and Human Resources department to learn about your options** if you must miss work to stay home with your caree.

14. **Check with current services that you use** (adult day centers, Meals on Wheels, volunteer programs, phone check-in programs, senior centers) and ask about their protocol during a weather emergency. Ask for their suggestions to fill any voids in care.

Long-Distance Caregiving: Tips for the Check-In Call

You live in New York City and your mom lives in Florida. You talk regularly. But, after each phone conversation, you wonder, How do I really know that all is okay?

Sometimes, caring conversations can be about the big issues (money, moving, a change in care needs) and sometimes it's about the little things, like how the day goes for your caree who lives a distance away. Caring conversations about the little things can help you understand when the bigger concerns (like when they need more help) need addressing.

During your conversations, ask questions to get a better understanding of your caree's day. It's not about peppering your caree with questions; it's about inserting good questions during your comfortable conversations.

Questions like these can help you gauge how well your caree manages:

- What's for dinner tonight?
- Where did you go yesterday?
- How do you organize your schedule so you take your medications on time?
- Who will you see today?
- What's the best part of your day?
- What's new in the neighborhood?
- Who called this week?
- What can I do for you?
- What have you been watching on TV?
- What's the gossip you're hearing lately?

Specific questions help you better understand your caree's situation. A general question, like "How are you feeling?" might be met with a general answer, "I'm doing fine," which really doesn't tell you much. Questions about what your caree eats and how often she goes grocery shopping help you understand how well she's managing. When she begins to struggle ("I haven't been able to get out shopping this week"), you can ask more questions to better understand the situation. Perhaps she didn't need groceries this week. Perhaps the trips to the grocery stores are beginning to wear her out.

When you understand what's going well, you can keep those things going well. When something starts to slip, you can begin to discuss alternatives. For instance, if the grocery shopping seems to be getting too hard, you can say, "Grocery shopping can be taxing. Let's look at options for having your groceries delivered."

When parents lived in their home, I lived close by, except when we had snow in Chicago. The few miles seemed like two hundred miles. When I knew the forecast called for snow, I called my parents the day before the expected snowfall and asked, "What's our game plan for the snow?"

A game plan meant I could plan my day to be available to shovel and my dad knew he could count on me to lend a hand. The game plan evolved to include a solution created by my dad. When the snow fall measured more than two inches, my dad would use a local handyman to plow his long driveway. These plans made the winter much easier for all of us. It all started with a friendly phone call.

Help Finding Quality Care

When you entrust your caree into the care of another, you wish for good care. When you begin the search for quality care, whether in the home or in the nursing home, you may wonder where to start. Begin with free tools available from Medicare.gov and ProPublica.org.

Home Health Compare, available at Medicare.gov, helps you when you're considering hiring in-home help through a Medicare-certified home care agency. A Medicare-certified agency will have nurses, physical therapists, occupational therapists, social workers and home health aides on staff.

The tool shares both results of patient surveys and the quality of patient care in five categories, including:
- Managing Daily Activities
- Managing Pain and Treating Symptoms
- Treating Wounds and Preventing Pressure Sores
- Preventing Harm
- Preventing Unplanned Hospital Care

Use Nursing Home Compare, also available at Medicare.gov, to learn about skilled nursing facilities in your or your family member's community. After entering your city or zip code, you'll receive the results of your search. You'll see an overall rating plus individual ratings for Health Inspections, Staffing and Quality Ratings. Facilities receive from one to five stars in each category; the more stars, the better. Nursing Home Compare bases its five-star rating on the annual state inspections of facilities; you can click to learn more about each facility, including when the last inspection took place and the inspection results. You also can compare a facility's rankings to the state and national averages.

Nursing Home Inspect, created by the non-profit journalism organization ProPublica, lets you dig into the details of recent nursing home inspections. According to ProPublica, "Our search engine looks through the narrative portion of the inspection reports — the part where inspectors describe conditions in the home and any deficiencies they discovered. This is where the details are." (Note that you also can request a copy of a facility's most recent inspection.) Before using Nursing Home Inspect, read its tip sheet, which will help you understand how to search effectively as well as how to understand your search results. This tool can be helpful as you decide between facilities because you'll have a better understanding of which facility meets your quality standards.

As you search, keep in mind that you are the best influence of quality care. Be active and involved in your caree's care–you are the most critical member of your caree's care team. Ask questions, be assertive about your concerns and follow-up to ensure care plans and treatments stay on track. Because of your involvement, your caree receives quality care.

Ensuring You Hire Quality Help

For the most part, you feel like you're managing your caree's care needs fairly well. Over time, you've created a routine that works for both of you. You also both understand your caree's care needs, which means providing them has become easier.

It's just the constant feeling of being on call that wears you out. If I could just have Saturday afternoons to myself, you think, I would feel better.

You begin to search for a home care worker who can stay with your caree while you take a break. You don't need the home care worker to provide care–you just need a professional to keep your caree comfortable and safe.

As you search for help, you realize that the agency which can provide what you need for your caree–companionship, supervision and light housekeeping–is not required to be certified through Medicare. Because the agency is not Medicare-certified, you can't research the agency to find its quality care rating through Medicare.gov's Home Health Compare database.

Without Home Health Compare, how do you know what kind of quality you're hiring?

Lee Lindquist, M.D., an associate professor of medicine at Northwestern University Feinberg School of Medicine and a physician at Northwestern Memorial Hospital, published research that indicated consumers, like you, must be cautious when hiring home care workers. To help you in your quest to find good help, Dr. Lindquist suggests you ask the following questions of any home care agency you interview:

1. How do you recruit caregivers and what are your hiring requirements?

2. What types of screenings are performed on caregivers before you hire them? Criminal background check—federal or state? Drug screening? Other?

3. Are they certified in CPR or do they have any health-related training?

4. Are the caregivers insured and bonded through your agency?

5. What competencies are expected of the caregiver you send to the home? Competencies could include lifting and transfers, homemaking skills, personal care skills such as bathing, dressing, toileting, training in behavioral management and cognitive support.

6. How do you assess what the caregiver is capable of doing?

7. What is your policy on providing a substitute caregiver if a regular caregiver cannot provide the contracted services?

8. If there is dissatisfaction with a particular caregiver, will a substitute be provided?

9. Does the agency provide a supervisor to evaluate the quality of home care on a regular basis? How frequently?

10. Does supervision occur over the telephone, through progress reports or in-person at the home of the older adult?

As you search for the right company to help you, ask family members and friends for recommendations of agencies they've used. And, listen to your gut–if it screams, then act or run, depending on what it screams.

Consider staying home the first time the home care worker will be with your caree. You can busy yourself in other parts of the house as you monitor how well the home care worker engages your caree.

Most important, you are the buyer of the home care agency's service. When you have concerns, contact the agency to discuss and resolve.

Ask Denise: How Do I Train My Replacement?

Dear Denise,

Finally, I'm going on vacation! I'll be gone for two weeks in September. My sister will stay at the house and take care of my mom.

Here's my problem: How in the world do I tell my sister what I do every day to take care of my mom?

Hello,

Good for you! It's wonderful you'll be able to take a well-deserved vacation.

Because you do so much, it can seem daunting to communicate so much, not only about what you do, but what your caree likes, dislikes, tolerates, can't tolerate. It's also hard to explain how you know how to manage your caree on a bad day--because it seems that you just know.

Some suggestions:

- I encourage family caregivers to keep two journals: One for their eyes only, about their experiences; the other, about their carees and their medical conditions. If you don't already keep journals, now's a good time to start. In particular, a journal about your caree will really be handy for your sister.
- In this second journal, document your caree's day: Meals, disagreements, hands-on care, challenges, moods, activities, and conversations. A good time to update this journal during the day is after every meal and after personal care (morning and night). Your sister can read your journal entries well before she takes over and she'll have time to ask questions or clarify information.

- Create a calendar that reflects your day's routine including bedtimes, medications, naps, meals, etc.

- Have your sister shadow you for a period of three days. Do this about two or three weeks before you're set to leave.

- A week or so after the shadowing, have your sister stay with you and your mom for a weekend. This time, though, she is the primary family caregiver. Schedule activities for yourself outside the house and alone so your mom and sister can start to develop their own routine. You'll be close by, though, in case of an emergency.

- Allow your sister to ask any "What if" questions she can think of, no matter how crazy or unrealistic they may be. Two questions I like to ask when I start a new job are "What's the worst mistake I can make?" and "What's the worst that can happen?" If I know the worst that can happen and have some solutions--just in case--then I know I'll be okay.

- Develop a back-up plan for your sister so that she'll have options if she becomes ill or encounters other emergencies.

- Be open to mistakes--from both of you. You always can re-group and move on. Keep your sense of humor and perspective and you'll be okay.

- Agree on your communication timetable while you're gone. Will you check in every day at a certain time? Will your sister call you every evening? What constitutes an emergency or a crisis and triggers a phone call to you? Meaning, how much do you want to know while you're gone?

- You can check with your local Area Agency on Aging and Red Cross to see if the agencies have any upcoming training classes for family caregivers. Additional training for your sister would be great.

The goal is to increase everyone's comfort level so that all three of you feel okay during your vacation. You also want to allow your sister and your mom the freedom to develop their own routines and habits. If it's different than how you would do it, that's okay.

I'm Enough, So I've Had Enough of the Doritos

On Your Caregiving Journey, my Internet talk show, Anna Stookey, a Beverly Hills-based therapist, joined me for a show called, "Ditching the Doritos." We talked about how to stop eating your way through a tough time.

We started our conversation with the recognition that eating can be the way we take a break. We're tired of caregiving. We're exhausted from phone calls. We're sick of trying to get help. So, we take a break, just 10 minutes. And, because we're stuck in the mode of action, we take a break with that bag of Doritos or that candy bar. When we finish the bag or the bar, we feel good—we accomplished something, which is often a feeling not enjoyed in caregiving.

Of course, the problem when we finish the bag or the bar is that soon enough we finish fitting into our clothes.

Ugh.

Anna suggested that we take meaningful breaks, including a break of doing absolutely nothing. Create a list of 20 or 30 ideas of activities you can enjoy during that 10-minute break. Your list may include:

1. Sit outside on the deck.
2. Call a friend.
3. Read a magazine or newspaper.
4. Visit CareGiving.com.
5. Draw a picture.
6. Take a photo.
7. Write a story about a recent caregiving experience.
8. Clip coupons.
9. Write in your journal.
10. Daydream.

Keep your list in a handy spot so you can refer to it before automatically reaching for the junk food.

We also spoke about the difference between physical hunger and emotional hunger. Anna offers a technique to help you better understand how to gauge your hunger. Describe how you feel when you're starving, like the stomach growls, you feel light-headed, you can't focus. On a hunger scale of 0 to 5, this would be a 5, the most hungry you'll feel. Then, consider what a 3 feels like and a 0. When you feel hungry, you can ask yourself, How hungry am I? Give your hunger a number to determine if you need food or some other kind of comfort or release. This is how your eating becomes mindful, a conscious decision.

We closed our show with an acknowledgment of the courage it takes to say "No" to more food or too much food. Often, we learn that eating (and eating too much) is the way we show love for others. We worry that saying "No" to food means we are hurting someone's feelings. We also may struggle with feeling full from food because we can't quite feel full in our lives. I think when we can tell ourselves, "I'm enough," we can feel more confident in saying, "I'm full."

So, know you are enough. Just as you are. You are enough.

Save the Wait for the DMV

We have a tendency to apply waiting lines in our life. Rather than walking up to the open window, we stand behind an invisible red line of our own creation.

We may wait to start a family until we have just the right house or the right amount in the bank.

We may wait to join a gym until we lose weight.

We may wait to change a job we hate until we have another set of skills or the seasons change like from fall to winter.

We can put ourselves in line to wait for what seem like good reasons. The truth is that our self-imposed waiting game helps us avoid facing a fear.

We fear we're not up to the responsibility of being parents so put off starting the family. We fear we may not look good enough so avoid the fitness center. We may fear the rejections that come with the job search so convince ourselves it's just not the right time.

During a caregiving experience, you may convince yourself it's okay to wait.

You may wait to get help believing it's not bad enough or hard enough or stressful enough. You may wait to learn about hospice services because, well, because. Who wants hospice?

You may fear how you look (incompetent, incapable) if you get help. You may fear your caree's disapproval if you get help. You may fear letting go (which means you are not completely in control) so you hold on too tight, leaving little room for help. You may fear using hospice believing that it's a form of giving up, that it means you aren't doing enough.

When we wait in life, we put our life on hold. When we wait during caregiving, we not only put our life on hold but set ourselves up for more and more stress. Without the right kind of help, we aren't capable of managing all that's required. Without enough help, we risk the well-being of ourselves and our carees. Without the right amount of help, we truly create chaos.

You may wait, believing it's not bad enough to have help. If you are helping, caring or worrying about a family member, it's always bad enough to get help. If you get help now, you understand how to work the help. You figure out the kind of help you need, who will help and who won't, what costs more than it should, what services are the best deal in town. When you get help early, you don't have to wait for help later. You don't have to wait to find services which lessen your stress, to understand how to approach your caree about using more help, to create a budget which represents the help you need.

When you have help early, you have help to manage those unexpected caregiving crises that you soon learn to expect.

The help could be joining a community support group which you only attend every few months. When you need more, you'll attend more. The help could be starting a blog, like on CareGiving.com, that you use to document the day. When bad days build, you'll have a release that's ready for you--your blog. Help could be hiring a home health aide that you use just once a month with the intention of adding more hours as your caree declines and care needs increase.

If you start adding help early, you can steadily increase the help in a way that's easier for you and your caree. Going from no help to a ton of help in a short time is hard on everyone. Because it's time consuming to find help, starting the search early means you'll have the time you need to find what truly helps.

A few years ago, I coached a client who regularly held off on getting more help. Every week during our coaching calls, she told me didn't need help. Each week as her mom's care needs increased, my client's will power waned, stress level increased and resentment built. Her kids suffered, her husband became frustrated and my client, interestingly enough, felt unsupported.

I consistently nudged (well, pushed) her to get more help. When she finally added more help and more help than she thought she needed, she had more time for her children, her husband and her own interests.

Why wait to feel better? In the waiting line, you won't feel better; you'll only feel impatience, frustration and intolerance.

You also may be tempted to wait to learn about hospice services. I often hear, "The doctor hasn't recommended hospice so we must not be ready." Waiting for a doctor to recommend hospice often can lead to the waiting game that just doesn't end until it's the end. And, then it's too late.

Learning about hospice providers in your community sooner rather than later can be one of the best waits you avoid. Finding the right hospice provider is just like finding any other good provider, like a home health agency or a nursing home.

You know what it's like when you add a new provider to the mix. It's new policies, procedures, paperwork. It's getting used to strangers, becoming comfortable with a new schedule. If you begin to use hospice services as soon as your caree qualifies, you understand the service and how it works so when you really need the support and help from hospice, it's there.

My client who regularly resisted getting help cared for her mom in her home. When her mom began to talk about death, I suggested my client talk to the doctor about hospice services. The hospice organization determined her mom was ready and provided services for eight months until her mom's death. Because my client began to use hospice months before her mom's death, she knew which nurses she liked and which ones she didn't. Because she knew which nurses she liked, she could request help from that nurse when she needed help. She felt comfortable calling the hospice staff with questions and concerns because she knew the hospice staff.

Now, imagine adding a provider, like hospice, during your caree's last week. Imagine getting acquainted with the staff and services. Why add that kind of stress during your caree's last week? You want the last weeks to be as comfortable for both of you as possible. When you add hospice as soon as your caree qualifies, you know how to use hospice services so you are both supported during that very critical time–the end.

So, how do you know when it's time for hospice? Contact hospice organizations when you begin to see the continual declines and ask. The staff can tell you about the criteria they use to determine eligibility. If your caree is not ready for hospice, then you've just bought yourself time. Most important, don't wait for your caree's doctor to tell it's time for hospice. You'll wait too long.

If you feel yourself waiting, do what you can to take action. Make a phone call, research options, ask for suggestions, try a service, talk out a worry with a friend, start journaling. Taking a step takes you out of fear. With each step, you'll feel more capable and confident.

During an experience like caregiving that reminds you regularly that we have finite time, don't wait. You don't have any time to waste.

"Never, never, never, never give up." ~ Winston Churchill

Stage III:
The Entrenched Caregiver

I am helping a family member or friend.

Who are you?

Your involvement with your caree is almost daily--if not constant. Your caree may live with you--or your involvement means that your day is structured to be available to your caree. You begin to wonder, how much longer can you live this way? Your mood is sometimes upbeat--you're proud you've been able to provide such wonderful care and make decisions that support your caree's best wishes. Sometimes you feel melancholy--why you? You've been mourning the loss of your caree's abilities and functions and often long for the days before caregiving. And, you're tired.

Your Keyword: Receive

--Receive help--from anyone who offers.
--Receive breaks from caregiving.
--Receive support.

Your Challenge

To find the support and strength to continue.

Your Purpose

To develop a routine, create a familiar schedule for both yourself and your caree. A routine will help you deal with the overwhelming stresses and responsibilities that wear you out. A routine will provide comfort for you and your caree--this stage may be the most difficult for both of you. The changes you prepared for in Stages I and II are now a reality--you have become a lifeline to a family member or friend.

In addition to your caree's routine of care, create a routine for yourself. In your routine include time to manage the unexpected that pops up during your day; a ritual which begins and ends your day; and a "healthness" activity to nurture your spiritual, emotional, physical and mental needs.

Judy and Frank

Frank continues to decline as a result of strokes and is now in a wheelchair. While her children wanted her to consider nursing home placement, Judy felt she owed it to Frank to care for him at home. She turned the dining room into his room because of its convenient location-- home care workers don't have to trudge through the house and up the stairs, home care equipment delivery (like his oxygen) is easy, and Frank remains close to all family functions when the children and grandchildren visit. Home health aides visit three times a week to help Judy, and her children provide respite on Sundays so that Judy can go to church and then out to lunch with friends.

Lately, her children have been asking Judy, "How much longer can you do this?"

Andy and Abigail

Abigail has moved from her home to a retirement community. Andy found a Realtor, sold the home and packed up his mother's belongings. He held garage sales during his week-long "vacation" at his mother's home. He helped his mother settle into the retirement community.

The move, although initially difficult, has been successful. Abigail has new friends and feels a new-found freedom without the burden of a large house. Andy continues to talk with Abigail daily for the next two years.

During this time, Andy notices that Abigail becomes more and more dependent on Andy, calling regularly to ask him what time it is, when her friends will meet her for lunch and what time the van will leave to take her and her friends shopping. As the calls increase in length and frequency, Andy finds himself becoming his mother's only connection to reality.

The social worker at the retirement community confirms that Abigail has exhibited signs of a dementia. At the social worker's urging, Andy schedules a physician's appointment for his mother and another trip home for a long weekend. The appointment confirms Andy's fears--his mother suffers from a dementia, possibly a result of mini-strokes.

Now, Andy has to face more decisions. The retirement community cannot provide the care that Abigail's dementia requires. The social worker indicates that Abigail can stay in the retirement community as long as she's able to make her way to the dining room for meals and manage her personal care. How long will that be, Andy wonders?

Andy keeps his siblings up-to-date on his mother's situation. They appreciate his updates, but tell him that they trust his decisions. He asks them to visit their mother; they refuse. After speaking with a sibling, he often closes his eyes and winces, as if they have caused him a physical pain. Because it feels so much like a physical pain.

As an "entrenched caregiver," what can you do?

1. Determine your limits in your day and in your role.

How long can your caree remain at home? What's your comfort level in providing care in your home? For instance, some family caregivers feel uncomfortable providing care when their caree becomes incontinent. Others determine they can provide care at home as long as insurance or Medicare benefits offset some of the home care expenses. Others feel they can provide care as long as their other family members, like spouses and adult children, will put up with it.

Just as important as understanding your limits in your role is recognizing your limits during your day.

Consider:

- Which tasks and responsibilities feel like a struggle?
- What times during the day do you feel the greatest amount of stress?
- When do you find yourself running late, losing your temper, scrambling for a solution?
- What do you find yourself dreading or hating?
- When do you find yourself in a tug-of-war with your caree?
- What times of the day are tough for your caree?
- When during the day does your worry about your caree intensify?

When you understand your limits, you can look for help to manage what's beyond your limits. Understanding your limits will ensure you, your caree and your family will stay in a safe place. Your limits aren't your failures but opportunities to put in place solutions to stay successful.

Everyone has limits. What are yours?

2. What are your caree's limits?

Understanding your caree's limits will help schedule your day and organize your help. Limits will change regularly, so be aware of change in tolerance and fatigue. Not sure how much help to schedule? Add more than you think. You can never have too much.

3. Continue regular breaks.

Consider annual weekly breaks--investigate short-term respite stays in your community's nursing homes. Or, ask relatives to take over the caregiving role for a week or two every year or every two years. Continue to take daily, weekly and monthly breaks, whatever you can manage.

Keep up with your own interests and hobbies as best you can. Take time to enjoy the paradise you built in Stage II.

A Stumble: Believing you are the only one who can provide the care your caree needs. So, when family members or friends offer to help out--feeding your caree, bathing your caree, or visiting with your caree--you politely decline. "Joe just likes me to be with him at mealtime," you say.

A Steady: You may be the best caregiver in your family, but you're not the only one. Sharing the experience helps your family grow, keeps your caree connected with others, and helps you maintain a healthy perspective.

4. Use your Solutions Fund. Make deposits and take withdrawals, using the money for boredom, breaks and back-up plans.

5. Keep up with a support system that reminds you that you are okay. Your support system could be a support group or your knitting circle. When you feel like you belong, you've found your support.

A Stumble: Because you are so tired and overwhelmed, you may forget how great it feels to unburden yourself. When others ask how you are doing, you say fine. When your best friend says, "Tell me what's bothering you?" You assure her you are okay.

A Steady: Discussing your concerns, your stresses and your burdens with a non-judgmental, caring listener will prove to be a weight-lifter. You'll feel pounds lighter and be able to view your caregiving role in a refreshed perspective.

6. Continue to learn about your caree's illness or condition.
What's next for your caree? Who and what can help you keep up with the next steps?

7. Increase help as your caree declines.
Become comfortable with adding more help as more help is needed. You may think, "I'm okay keeping the level of help as it is." Unfortunately, keeping the level where your caree *was* rather than where he or she *is* will hurt both of you. Note the struggles in the day, then work to add help for you and your caree to manage the struggles.

8. Manage the budget as much as you manage the care.
As care needs increase, so does the budget. When you caree has funds to pay for about 18 months in a nursing home, then take note of the situation. This is the time to consider nursing home placement, when your caree's funds will afford the best choices. Hold a family meeting, tour local facilities, consult with professionals, such as an aging life care specialist or Certified Caregiving Consultant. You may decide this isn't the time to decide. That's okay. It's important to be aware that sometimes the budget determines the decision on where a caree continues to receive care. It's most important to be aware of your choices and to make the one that's right for you and your caree.

   If you care for your spouse and consider nursing home placement, know that a certain amount of your assets will be protected and that you will not have to deplete all your assets to pay for your spouse's care in a nursing home. Visit Medicaid.gov and search for "spousal impoverishment" to learn more.

9. Continue writing in both journals—yours and the other about your caree.

10. Forgive yourself for your bad moments and bad days.
They will happen. After they do, give yourself a clean slate to start over.

11. Set boundaries which protect your time, your values, your well-being, your priorities and your self. Examples of communicating boundaries include:
   - "I'm taking a two-hour break after lunch. I have everything that you'll need set up in the living room. Thank you so much for helping me enjoy this time. I'm so grateful for your support."

   - "I'm uncomfortable with the tone of our discussion. Let's table our talk until tomorrow."

   - "I'm booked, so have to decline. Thank you for thinking of me."

   - "I'm only available to take your phone calls between 6 p.m. and 8 p.m. If you call after 8 p.m., I'll let your call go to my voice mail and I'll call you back when I can."

12. Give you and your caree room for your difficult moments and bad days.
When you're having a tough time, simply say, "I'm having a bad day. I'm

taking a few minutes for myself." When it's your caree's turn, say, "I'm sorry you're having a bad day. I'm going to step away for a few moments."

13. An apple a day…
What's your apple in this stage? You may feel tempted to sacrifice your apple in this stage. Your apple can't be sacrificed. Your apple is what makes you feel normal, like yourself. Keep it.

A Quick Tip:

In order to survive a trying and emotionally-charged experience, we need to find the meaning. Your experience as a family caregiver is meaningful. You can find the meaning when:

--You receive help for yourself and your caree from community organizations, your house of worship, your family members, your caree's friends and neighbors. Regular breaks mean you can gain a healthier perspective.

--You allow yourself and your caree to feel the emotions of the experience. Is your caree angry that she has had to leave her own home? Allow her to tell you about it. Do you miss your old life--its action, its freedom, its spontaneity? Allow yourself to vent your frustration in a healthy way in your journal, to your support group, in your artwork.

--You accept the imperfections of the experience and of the people in the experience, including yourself. Accept that this journey is about helping a family member or friend live as well as possible until death arrives, whether that be in 25 years or 25 days. Accept that the journey will have many difficult moments. Accept that you can have just as many good moments. And, accept that people may not be able to step up in the way you want. As Maya Angelou says, "The first time someone shows you who they are, believe them." Accept that help will come from unusual and expected sources.

Most important, it's okay. You're okay. When you receive, allow and accept, you make room for meaningful moments between you and your caree. That's when you find the meaning of your caregiving journey.

The Entrenched Caregiver
Your Reflections

In this stage, what are your goals?
—For your caree?

—For you and your family?

How will you achieve these goals?

Who can help you achieve these goals?

What overwhelms you?
—In caring for your caree?

—In caring for you and your family?

How can you unload some of the burdens?

The Entrenched Caregiver
Your Resource Library

...ioning from Some Help to More Help

...gue recently asked me to lunch. "I want to pick your brain about
...ents," she said.

I knew some of her parents' history--they lived in a rural area on the East
Coast. My friend lived in Chicago while her siblings resided on the West
Coast. I also knew her parents had been resisting help. I knew we were
going to talk about how to get her parents to accept more help.

And, we did. Her mother, diagnosed with dementia, struggled more with
her short-term memory loss. Her father, older than his wife by seven
years, was now slowing in his ninetieth decade.

I'm going for a visit soon, my friend said. What can I do to help them?
It's a smart idea to plan ahead to take advantage of an upcoming trip to
visit parents or other aging relatives. You can use the time together wisely
to begin the transition to more help.

These suggestions can help you make the most of a visit:

**1. If your caree suffers from short-term memory loss, call the local
chapter of the Alzheimer's Association for a list of physicians and
clinics which can diagnose dementia.** A primary care physician can be a
great resource, but when it comes to the tricky business of diagnosing
dementia, you'll want a team of specialists to run a battery of tests. You'll
want to schedule the appointment during your visit so you hear the
diagnosis and recommendations. Large hospital systems often will have
clinics, sometimes called Memory Clinics, which specialize in diagnosing
and treating Alzheimer's and related dementias. The National Institutes of
Health provides funding to Alzheimer's Disease Centers across the
country. There aren't enough, but it's a start.

2. Understand the resources available to you. It turns out my friend's
parents have a neighbor who worked for a local home care agency. The
neighbor can be a knowledgeable source of information about local
community services.

3. Build on what's already working. My friend kept insisting her parents
wouldn't accept any help. About an hour into our conversation, she

mentioned her parents had a housekeeper who cleaned once a week. My friend (and her siblings and her uncle) has been nagging her parents to get a new housekeeper. Ah!, I said, use the idea of a new housekeeper to add more help in the house. Perhaps rather than hiring another housekeeper, hire a home health aide, which can help with light housekeeping, meal preparation and personal care. I've often found that something is working which keeps a caree home. Figure out what that secret sauce is and then build on it.

4. Be a part of the transition. I suggested that my friend schedule appointments to interview help during her visit. When she's a part of the interview and hiring process, she can help her parents continue with the transition. If she's not there, it's easier for her parents to say, "We didn't find anyone we liked." With my friend a part of the process, she can offer words of encouragement to her parents like, "I know this is tough. We can figure out how to make this work together."

5. Experience the change together. After hiring more help, I suggested that my friend or another family member be involved when the new help arrives. When you understand the impact of the change, you can take steps to make adjustments so your caree isn't undone by the change. When bumps happen, and they will, your perspective can help calm rough waters. You also can quickly contact the agency to address concerns before they become huge problems.

6. Create back-up plans. The irony of involving more help is that it solves some problems but can create new ones. Help will cancel, get sick, find new jobs. Once you've organized more help, work on a back-up plan. Find another home health agency who can provide staff in a pinch. Learn about other community service providers and organizations which can help. A plan of care evolves and adjusts as a caree's needs change and as availability of help changes.

The move into more help and care can be an unsettling time for everyone. With a plan, you can feel better about managing the experience for all of you.

My Caree Won't Cooperate!

You've finally decided the time has come. You need help in your caregiving role and you'd like to hire a home health aide to help with your caree's personal care. With your job, your kids, your spouse and your other commitments, you've discovered it's just impossible to do it all yourself. Amazingly, it's a relief to come to this decision.

Until you think about breaking the news to your caree. You know the news won't be welcomed with open arms and neither will the home care worker.

Worrying about the tussle between you and your caree about getting help can cause you to re-think your decision to get help. It's tempting to give in to guilt but, in the long run, you'll jeopardize your caree's health and safety without the help.

If a caree refuses help in the house, work to get a commitment to use in-home care on a trial basis. For instance, when your caree says, "I will not have strangers in my house!," you might try this approach:

"Mom, I can understand your concerns about strangers in the house. I think you're wise to be skeptical that this will work. I also worry about you and want you to be safe at home. What if we try this? Let's try using a home health aide for a month. I'll be with you the first few times the aide comes. We'll have her come three days a week for four hours. I'll make sure you have a notebook and pen so you can jot down notes about the aide and how it's working out. I'll still call you every day, but we'll set aside Saturday mornings just to discuss the aide. I'll stop by to have coffee with you and we'll go over your notes. What do you say? Can we try this for a month and see how this works?"

It's important to get a commitment on a trial basis because often it's the springboard to a permanent commitment. If you take time to listen to your caree's complaints, you may be able to solve small problems before they become huge problems and huge barriers to a permanent commitment. If, when you have your Saturday morning meeting, your caree shares complaints that concern you, then you can contact the home care agency immediately on Monday morning to resolve them.

When introducing the idea of in-home care or any new service to your caree, keep in mind these tips:

1. Listen for the meaning behind the words. Is your caree angry, sad, depressed? Love and fear are our two motivating emotions and, most times, we act out of love or fear. It's easy to see actions from love. Actions from fear are trickier, though, because the fear can manifest itself in anger or guilt. Those can be very difficult emotions to deal with. When you hear anger, understand your caree may be experiencing fear.

2. Once you've understood the message, then acknowledge your caree's feelings. An acknowledgment can sound like this: "It's absolutely understandable why you would so angry and upset, Mom. How can I help?" Acknowledging means you've heard your caree and that's a great way to bridge communication. We all want to be heard.

3. Involve a third-party, a trusted professional or family friend, who can help mediate discussions with your caree. Physicians, lawyers and ministers or rabbis often can help smooth rough waters with your caree. Bad news is often best delivered from a third-party, rather than from you.

4. You may feel that you wear a t-shirt with a bulls-eye at which your caree is constantly taking aim. Take off the t-shirt! If discussions become verbally abusive, end the phone conversation, walk away, take a walk, escape to your room. Remember that the disease and illness and sometimes the caree's disposition and circumstances are to blame—not you.

5. Give back some control. Be sure your caree has some control, when appropriate, over the decisions about care.

6. Show gratitude with words and action. Give your caree a hug and say, "Thank you for being such a trooper. It's great to be on the same team with you. Who knows what we can do together?" Positive words often create positive actions.

7. We all adjust to changes at our own pace. Your caree may need more time to adjust than you. That's okay. Take one step a time.

8. Bad moments during the adjustment are just that—bad moments. Don't give the bad moments the power to become bad weeks and months. When your caree has bad moments, love him or her through them, as Dr. Phil would say.

9. Be flexible in the strategies you use to help your caree with the transition. Some will work, some won't. If a strategy doesn't work, try something else. Think outside the box. Ask others for suggestions and ideas. Focus on your efforts, rather than on trying to control an outcome you think is right. When you keep your attention on your efforts, you control what can be controlled—you. Trying to control an outcome, which is trying to control your caree, will only frustrate and exhaust you.

10. Take breaks from the situation. Breaks will refresh you and provide you with different perspectives. During a difficult transition, you may feel like spending time with your caree is like sitting in front of the TV watching a barrage of bad news. When you take a break, you take a break from the bad news. You give yourself a chance to see the good news, to see what's working and to regain a confident footing.

11. Focus on the expectations you have of your own behavior. What behavior do you feel is acceptable when your caree tries to lay a guilt trip on you? How would you like to react when your caree tries to manipulate you?

12. Recognize what you can control. You can't control your caree but you can control what knowledge you have of the disease and of what programs and services can help. Staying informed of options and solutions helps.

13. Forgive you and your caree your bad days. You both are humans operating under challenging and difficult circumstances.

14. Keep your sense of humor. When you can laugh and, even better, laugh with your caree, you'll keep your perspective.

Finally, have a back-up plan in place. If your caree won't accept help, still contact home health agencies, adult day centers and facilities in your caree's community. Meet with the staff to learn about services and programs so you'll know which ones will best meet you and your caree's needs. If an emergency happens, you'll know which organizations will help. When your caree is ready to accept help, you'll be ready with the right organization.

Sometimes, It's Not a Responsibility But an Opportunity

I had a coaching client a few years ago who did whatever she could to keep the responsibility of caregiving off the shoulders of her husband and her three children. Her mother's care, she decided, was a burden she must carry alone.

Except she couldn't, especially because the six of them shared a home. Trying to compartmentalize the burden meant she isolated her mom, creating invisible walls she hoped sealed her mom and her declines from the family. Her husband and her children took their cue from my client–disengaging from their mother-in-law and grandmother. The six spent much of the caregiving experience splintered.

When her mom began her final decline, my client focused on spending as much time as possible with her. During her mom's last week, she canceled most of her appointments outside the house, except for one she couldn't. Her husband encouraged her to go the support group meeting she led while he got dinner together for the kids.

It also meant he had to give dinner to his mother-in-law.

Her husband assured my client he would be fine and that she should go. And so he sat with his mother-in-law, feeding her dinner, placing a bite of food on a fork that he placed in her mouth.

It was the last meal she ate. She died six days later.

My client worried so much about unloading a responsibility that she inadvertently withheld an opportunity. At her mother's memorial, my client's oldest daughter, a teenager of 16, regularly said to her mom, "I should have done more to help."

When her husband reflects on the 10 years his mother-in-law lived with his family, he can take pride and comfort in knowing he helped at the end. Thank goodness for the chance he had to spend those moments, moments of tenderness and love, with his mother-in-law. He has a story of how he cared.

Sometimes, we just don't have others with whom we can share the caregiving experience. When we do, it's important to remember that sometimes we're not off-loading a responsibility but instead creating an opportunity for comforting memories to last a lifetime. When we look back, we want to remember that we did, in our way, contribute to the difference.

Is This Normal?

Caregiving stirs up so many emotions—emotions sometimes too embarrassing to acknowledge. You may wonder: Is this normal?

Answer "yes" or "no" to each statement, below, to determine how normal your caregiving experience is.

1. I often long for the days prior to my caregiving role.
2. On a regular basis, I fight to maintain my composure.
3. Sometimes, I just dread interacting with my caree.
4. I often think I am not doing enough.
5. I feel shame about my emotions, particularly the resentment and anger.
6. I have wished that my caregiving days would end.
7. I have hidden from my caree (in another room, in my car, in the bathroom).
8. I am not the person I was.
9. I have lost my temper.
10. I am really, really tired.

Did you answer yes to any of the questions? To all of them?

Guess what? You're normal!

Caregiving can test you unlike an other life experience. The emotions associated with a caregiving experience can be so negative, even if you really, really love your caree. These emotions can wear you down faster than the transfers you make from the bed to commode. To stay well emotionally, allow yourself regular opportunities to vent. You may feel guilty about sharing how you really feel. That's normal, too. Work through the guilt so you can express your frustrations to a safe and understanding audience, whether it be your support group, your journal or your close friend.

If you keep it in, it will do you in.

Quiz: Is Your Blow-Up Around the Corner?

Caregiving can test your patience like no other life experience. Day after day, it seems that caregiving chips away at your patience, bringing you closer and closer to a blow-up.

How close are you? Take our quick test to find out.

A. Your mother calls you to her room for the umpteenth time in 10 minutes. You know what she'll ask before you reach her doorway. Sure enough, you find her in her bedroom, ruffling through her nightstand drawer. "Yes, Mom," you say, in your calmest possible voice. "What do you need?"

Your mom turns around and says, "I need my Rosary. That's what I need. What did you do with it?"

You:

1. Say, "Mom, we've been through this 20 times already today. I don't know where it is. I didn't take it. You'll just have to find it yourself" and leave the room. Thirty minutes later, you check back on your mom and find her room in disarray. An hour later, you've put her room back in place—and forgot to pick up your daughter from school.

2. Say, without a twinge of guilt, "Susie (your sister, your mom's favorite) took it. I don't know why she keeps taking your Rosary from you. She knows how important it is to you. I would never do that." (Serves Susie right, you think, as you head out the door. She never helps, she might as well take some of the blame.) This, of course, becomes the only thing your mom remembers all day. She follows you from room to room asking, "Why doesn't Susie love me? Why would she take my Rosary?"

3. Help her find it. You say, "I know how important the Rosary is to you," you say. As you move things around in the drawer, you place one of the replacement Rosaries you keep handy in the drawer. You let your mom find it. "There it is," you say. "I'm so glad you found it. Let's go in the kitchen and make some tea."

B. Your husband starts bellowing for you. "Take this oxygen tank outside," he says. "I'm going to have a cigarette."
You:

1. Take the oxygen tank outside, but make as much noise as you can and ding as many walls as you possible. You stand outside with the oxygen tank for 30 minutes (this will show him!!, you think) and, once you feel frostbite take hold of your fingers, drag the tank back inside. Your husband looks up from the paper as you bang, ding and swing the tank back into the living room. "You put some dents in the wall," he says as he calmly points to the living room wall. "You'll have to paint and spackle tomorrow."

2. You scream and stomp one foot, then another. "You can't smoke!! You can't smoke!! I'm calling the doctor!" You call the doctor's office; as a result of your phone call, the doctor prescribes Valium—for you.

3. You say, "I think we'll keep the oxygen tank in here. I'll open the door for you so you can go outside and smoke."

C. You finally are out of the house because your neighbor volunteered to stay with your caree while you run to the grocery store. You've run out of hard candy, the only thing that seems to keep your caree calm in the afternoons. Sucking on the hard candy seems to keep her distracted, keeping her late afternoon agitation at bay. On your way to the store, an older driver pulls in front of you, almost causing an accident.

You:

1. Lay on the horn, which keeps blowing and blowing and blowing and… You applied so much pressure it seems you've stuck your horn. You drive to the store and all the way with your horn blowing. In addition to the hard candy, you also bring home a splitting headache.

2. Without thinking, you raise a particular finger which relays a particular message. And, then because you know the driver is probably hard of hearing, you roll down your window and yell, "Don't you know how to drive?? Get off the road!" Ten minutes later, the guilt is so great about the finger and the screaming that you purchase the wrong hard candy at the store. It's a long evening for you and your caree.

3. Say a quick "Thanks," with a look to the sky, that no one was hurt as you change lanes. "I think I'll take the long way home," you say to no one in particular. You call home and speak to your neighbor: "It's such a nice day," you say, "that I'm going to take 15 minutes to sit in the park." "Good for you," your neighbor says. "Enjoy!"

D. Your spouse is having a bad day today so you're having one, too. No matter what you do or how you do it, it's not right. Now, she wants lunch and is requesting the very meal you don't have.

You:

1. Run out to the store and buy what she wants. Inside, you're cursing her. You call your daughter and say, "I can't stand your mother today. You'll have to come here and take over." Your daughter arrives and takes advantage of the opportunity to lecture you. "I can't keep rescuing you," she says. "If you can't handle this, we'll have to talk about nursing home placement."

2. Fix the meal you had planned. You're so burned up about her lack of gratitude that you burn lunch in the process. You tell her, "Too bad! It's what we have, so it's what you're getting." You and your spouse spend the rest of the day in silence. The silence lingers overnight and into the next day.

3. Stop for a minute to take a few deep breaths. "Let's sit and talk for a minute," you say to your spouse. "What's going on today? We're having such a bad day. I love you too much to spend a bad day with you. How can we make it a good one?"

How did you do?
Mostly 1's: The bad news: You're angling for a blow-up. The good news: It hasn't happened yet. Take as much time on your own as you can; whether it be at night after your caree has gone to bed, or early in the morning before your caree gets up. Give yourself a break from some scheduled activities when you can. Your rest is the top priority. Continue to vent and rant to your support system because letting it out to them is healthy.

Mostly 2's: The bad news: You've had your blow-up. The good news: What goes up, must come down. Give yourself a break, let anything but the most important caregiving responsibilities go. Call in the reserves, schedule extra help, go to bed early, get up late—whatever you can manage. Everyone has blow-ups. Move on, but be sure you move on by taking some important time to yourself. Look to your support system to share those bad days as those who get it often can turn a bad day into something that's amazingly not so bad.

Mostly 3's: The good news: You're in good shape! The bad news: The challenge is keeping yourself in good shape. Give yourself time, even if you feel you don't need it. Continue to participate in your support system because they'll be great to have on your bad days.

When the Bombs Drop (and They Will)...

Many years ago, a member of one of our online support groups regularly reminded the group members that life is for the living.

In caregiving, you sometimes feel stuck between life and death. How do you go about life when death and decline won't go away?

I'm reminded of a documentary I watched of life in London during WWII. In the film, we saw how Londoners managed during the war, when bombings became a normal part of living. The Blitz (sustained German bombing) occurred from September 7, 1940 until May 10, 1941, with smaller attacks continuing until the war ended.

We saw footage of London devastation—lives lost, homes ruined, a city rubbled. We also saw footage of Londoners walking around the wreckage as they went about their days shopping, sending their children to school and even attending a dance.

They never stopped living, even as death and destruction surrounded them.

For you, caregiving can seem like another kind of blitz. You get bombed and bombarded by bad news, unsuccessful treatments, continual losses, sadness.

During the bombings, you may catch yourself thinking, "I'd better pass on that bit of fun. Our life is just not so good right now." You may think enjoying life means disrespecting the seriousness of your life.

On the contrary.

You sacrifice so much. Don't sacrifice a moment to laugh or to dance or to simply smile. These are moments given to you, just for you. Take them and then share them.

If the Londoners could do it, you can, too.

Finding the Fluid Motion of Priorities

I recently heard someone say that we human beings like structure and order. When something does not make sense, we look for and sometimes create explanations.

During times of stress and uncertainty, when nothing makes sense, I wonder what life is really about.

I asked a friend, "Is life about sacrifices? Do we sacrifice so ultimately we can get what we want?"

"Absolutely not," she answered. "Anyone who makes a life out of sacrifices is simply a martyr. I don't believe any Higher Being would want our lives to be about sacrifices."

"Then is life about compromises?" I asked. "Do we compromise, taking the bad with the good, to get what we want?"

"No, it's not about that, either," she replied. "Compromises can be a part of life, but it's not what life is."

After pondering this for a night, I wondered if our priorities could be the answer.

When difficult times come our way, do we survive by re-prioritizing and by making sure our pressing needs top our to-do list? Is prioritizing a survival instinct? Do we prioritize or perish?

I do believe we continue by prioritizing. I also think our challenge becomes understanding that our priorities can change as our life and our life's circumstances change.

We tend to put the pressing needs at the top of our list. Our caree certainly has significant, sometimes critical, needs. As caregiving lasts from one year to the next and into the next, we can't keep going in a healthy way if our life revolves around only one priority. Others we love must be priorities, too, otherwise we sacrifice those relationships.

We also can make ourselves a priority once in awhile. We practice this by making ourselves a priority for a minute by taking several seconds to close our eyes and breathe. We then expand those seconds into a few minutes by stepping outside to take in nature's sights and sounds. When we feel comfortable with those few moments, we can turn them into a few hours. We might hire a home health aide to be with our caree so we can spend a few hours at the local library.

Our perspective on our priorities will shift during our caregiving experience. Any time we shift, we need time to adjust. An adjustment may be painful as we work through our own guilt and others, like our caree, resist our shift. Rather than giving up because the adjustment hurts, we can commit to the process of discovering our priorities and their timing.

We can think of our priorities as a series of actions rather than as a list written in permanent marker. A priority at any given moment in time can be:

> Achieving
> Being
> Believing
> Caregiving
> Enjoying
> Loving
> Receiving
> Resolving

In this moment, your priority may be receiving this information. In the next hour, your priority may be enjoying time with your kids or grandkids. After that priority, caregiving may be the focus.

Fluid priorities become simple motions within our day. Our priorities aren't about choosing one over the other but about embracing the opportunity we have right now to make the most of what is.

When we give ourselves permission to look at our priorities as flexible pieces in our puzzle, we give ourselves a fighting chance during a tough time. We continue.

Quiz: Are You On Overload?

Well, sure, of course, you are. You're worried, worn-out, weathered. You may also be way over your limit in terms of what you're doing. Take our quick quiz to find out how much you are over on your load.

1. It's the fifth time you must take your caree to the doctor this month. You're not sure how you're going to manage to pick up your caree, get to the doctor, take your caree home and all during your lunch hour from work.

a. You ask your sister to take the day off and accompany your mom. You call your sister five times the night before and six times the morning of the appointment to make sure she'll remember to pick up your mom. By 11 a.m., you're so exhausted from worrying you fall asleep in your cube and wake up three hours later but only because your boss is shaking you, hard, by the shoulders.

b. You run out of the office at 11:30, drive home, get your caree, arrive at the doctor's office, wait, accompany your caree into the appointment (but forget to ask your questions because you're too busy watching the clock), schedule a follow-up appointment with the nurse on your way out, then breathe a sigh of relief as you realize you'll just make it back to the office on time after dropping off your caree at home. "That wasn't too bad," you turn and say to your caree. Horror fills you. The passenger in your car has white hair but that isn't your caree!

c. You call the home care agency and arrange for a home health aide to bring your caree. You call the doctor's office, find out if the doctor is running behind schedule (surprise!, he is), explain to the office nurse that a home health aide will bring your mother today, and then schedule a time tomorrow to speak with the doctor about the appointment. You then call home and update the aide on the status of the appointment.

2. Your out-of-town brother calls and says, "I took a week off work to come stay with Grandpa so you can get away." After you pick yourself up from the floor:

a. You book a hotel room five minutes from home. You know your brother will need your help.

b. You tell him, "I don't need a week off. Thanks, but that's not necessary."

c. Spend one day acclimating your brother to your caree's needs and routines. Then, you hit the highway. You've been dreaming and planning about such a road trip for months.

3. A good friend invites you to dinner and a movie (his treat). During the movie that you've been dying to see:

a. You excuse yourself every 20 minutes to call home and make sure all is okay with your caree.

b. You sleep. You snore so loudly you wake yourself up.

c. You enjoy. Afterward, you invite your friend out for dessert–your treat.

4. You invite your caree's best friend, Pat, for dinner.

a. You worry so much about how Pat will react to your caree's change in condition that you hover over the two of them, so much so that Pat finally loudly whispers to your caree, "How do you get any privacy around here?"

b. You serve your caree's pureed meal to your caree and, unfortunately, to Pat. You don't realize this until you clear the dishes.

c. Make a simple meal and then excuse yourself. You've rented a good movie to enjoy while your caree is occupied.

How did you do?
Mostly A's: You're nearing overload. It's okay to trust that others can care for your caree. It won't be your same loving care, but it will be okay. You'll be okay, too.

Mostly B's: You're on overload! Stop–whatever you're doing. Sit, rest and let yourself off the hook. You're not meant to be perfect. You're only meant to do your best and you are. Remember that you can plan but you can't control. Put your plans in place. What happens while you take time for yourself is beyond your control. Let it go.

Mostly C's: Hurray, you're in good shape. Stay in shape by taking advantage of any and all opportunities to share the load.

Taking the Edge Off Socializing

It took a few years but you've finally got a caregiving system down. You have a home health aides you and your caree like, an adult day center your mother will attend, and a brother who will help foot the bill. Now, you finally have time to go out and socialize with friends.

It should be great but why does it feel so awkward?

You hear it all the time. Get out! Take a break from caregiving! It's great in theory, but sometimes the outside world can be scarier than caregiving. If you've been inside concentrating on caregiving and not necessarily keeping up with the rest of the world, well, once you get out, you may want to run back in.

If you've been out of circulation, re-entering the social scene can be awkward, scary and confusing. The world may have changed while you were doing load after load of laundry. Understanding how you fit within the changes can take time.

Being out of the house means being out of your comfort zone. There's nothing like simple questions about your complicated life to increase your discomfort. To help you gain confidence, bring our suggested answers with you to avoid feeling tongue-tied:

1. "What's new?"

This seems like such an easy question, but in the world of caregiving, the answer is always complex. A few ideas on how to answer:

--"We're all doing well." If the questioner is an acquaintance, it might be easier to provide general answers. And, even if you're not all doing well, sometimes it feels better to say you are.

--"Mom is having a bad week, but I'm doing okay. And, I'm so glad to be here with you today!" If the questioner is a friend or good friend, this answer works great. You've told the truth, but then moved on to your goal to enjoy your time out of the house.

--"With Alzheimer's, there's always something new! This week, the dog is new. But, overall, Frank is doing okay and I'm glad to have some time with you today. I've been looking forward to it all week."

--"I'm out of the house—that's what new! Let's start the fun!"

2. "What do you do?" (i.e., What's your career? Are you working?)

All too often, society equates one's worth with a great career. Remember, caregiving is not for the faint of heart so don't downplay what you do.

--"My mom needs help these days. So, I'm taking care of her. Because I'm her caregiver, I'm thinking about a new career when I can get back out working. So, right now, I'm taking online classes toward a nursing degree."

--"I'm home with my husband, who has Alzheimer's disease. Are you working?" Providing a short answer and then asking a question can help deflect any awkwardness you may feel.

--"I'm raising my family and taking care of my parents. Two full-time jobs! But, I'm still walking and talking, although my friends often ask me how I do it. How about you?"

--"I left the corporate world to take care of my parents. It was a tough decision, but one I'm very proud of. How about you?"

Consider that, in social interactions, a good listener is highly valued because there aren't many good listeners left in the world. If you find yourself without any words, then go ahead and listen. Smile and nod and then ask questions when you feel comfortable. When you find common ground, share something about yourself. Your listener will be in awe at what he or she discovers about you.

When you start socializing again, give yourself time to find your comfort zone, to find your way. Small steps will lead to social success allowing your caregiving world and your break from the caregiving world to co-exist peacefully.

In or Out? On the Bad Days of Caregiving

Liz has a debate going on in her head and a torment going on in her heart. It's been a bad day and not for any particular reason that Liz can pinpoint. It could be that her youngest will turn 10 soon. Or that next week her mom will be living with them for three years. Or that her husband will leave for another week-long business trip in a few days. Or it could be all three.

It's been a day that's kept her eyes full of tears.

Now, it's 7 p.m. and Liz should leave for her book club meeting in a few moments. She loves her monthly book club meeting and usually can't wait to get there. But, leaving for a book club means opening up the possibility that the very nice librarian who runs the book club will say, "Liz, is everything okay?"

How in the world do I respond without just sobbing, Liz thinks.

On those bad days, do you stay in? Take a chance and go out?

A few suggestions as you consider what's best for you:

1. Sometimes, a change of scenery can make a huge difference. The act of getting ready—a shower and fresh clothes—can help.

2. Focusing on another task or responsibility can take your mind off your sadness. It can be a nice break to think about something else.

3. The worry over how to answer the simple question, "Are you okay?", may make you think twice about leaving the house. Having a ready answer may help you feel like you can be in control. "I'm struggling today," you can explain, "but I want to take my mind off that and it's important for me to be here." Then, take a deep breath and say, "Thank you. I'm feeling better already."

4. Call a good friend. Let it out. Explain that you have an important engagement you'd like to attend but you're not feeling up to it. Then, just talk it out.

5. Write it out. Write that you don't feel well, that you worry about crying in front of others, that you want to take some time for yourself and enjoy it but can't convince yourself that it's possible. Write out the pros and cons of leaving the house. Sometimes, the pen can provide a perspective.

6. When tomorrow arrives, what will you wish you would have done today? Thinking into your future can sometimes propel you forward in your present.

7. Allow yourself the freedom to go and then return home if it's all just too much. If it does become too much, you can simply say, "I'm having a bad day today. I usually love being here which is why I came. But, I think I would do better at home. Thanks for understanding." Leaving is absolutely okay. You know what's best for you.

Sigh. If Only It Was Vomit

Stacey stood in line at the pharmacy. Actually, she jumped up and down in line at the pharmacy. She shouldn't be here, she should be at home. But her siblings won't return her calls, her husband is out of town and her father is in need of his refills.

She waited until the last minute, but she waited hoping, hoping, hoping that someone could run this errand for her. She needs to be at home.

So, while she waits, she jumps. Her anxiety seems to propel her up and down. It's like she's stuck in the ball that the gerbil at home spins in his cage—moving all around but stuck. Stuck in line. When she needs to be home.

Before she knows it, it's like she has an out-of-body experience. She hears herself yelling at the pharmacist, who inexplicably chooses this day to work in slow motion. "What's taking so long," she hears herself shout. "Why can't you move faster? The service here sucks!"

It's only then, after the words leave her mouth, that she realizes the slow-motion pharmacist is actually her favorite pharmacist, the one who diligently and kindly explains why each medication has been prescribed, what side effects to watch for, and how to dispense each one (with or without meals, without grapefruit juice, etc.). The pharmacist who any other day feels like her best friend in the whole word.

Oh, no, she thinks, I just spewed. If only it were vomit instead of words.

Now what?

You hope to avoid moments that lead to a spew. You do your best to relax regularly by listening to relaxation tapes, participating in an online support group, writing in your journal. Even with your best efforts, caregiving can get the best of you. How do you clean up after a spew?

A few suggestions:
1. Apologize.
2. Apologize again.

3. Quietly slip away.

It's these kinds of days when memory problems seem like problem-solvers. Oh, to be able to forget.

Do your best to do just that—forget. Let go and give yourself a chance for better. Gain from this experience by putting in place a regular way to vent so the steam releases over time rather than in one giant eruption.

When You Accept, You Gain

Caregiving is a journey of acceptance.

Think about the first thing you accepted in your caregiving role: A diagnosis.

The diagnosis led to worries. "Do I have enough?" you may have thought. It's a worry that stays. You worry if you'll have enough money, help, resources, information and support. You worry if you'll know what to do and how to do it.

You worry about life without your caree and how you'll manage.

Then, once the diagnosis sinks in, you begin to see the bigger picture, which leads to more worries about what you'll lose, like freedom, money, opportunities, travel, friends, fun.

Then resistance arrives. "I like how my life is," you may think. "I don't want anything to change."

As you worry and resist, time marches on, leaving you in the past.

Then, you become really attached to all the drama created from worrying and resisting, like:

- Self pity
- Excuses not to do
- Excuses not to handle.

Oh, that drama can deceive, leading you to believe the self-pity and excuses are reasonable. Worse than deceiving, the drama can lead to the the village of martyrdom. The drama tricks you into sacrificing too much of your life and of yourself until you feel absolutely empty.

Still you resist. Because if you accept what life has become, you feel you will lose. You may lose:

- an expectation of your future
- a reason to be upset

- a protective shield
- the right to be right
- the way it was yesterday
- an opportunity to judge
- the sympathy from others
- your own self-pity
- the good life you shared with your caree.

You may think: "If I accept this diagnosis, then I may lose the love I share with my caree."

Or:

"If I accept my siblings' limitations, then I may lose the opportunity to sit in judgment and feel superior."

Or:

"If I accept more help, then I may lose my significance."

You hold on, believing any other action will be a loss.

The best way to manage a loss, like the ones that come with caregiving, is through acceptance. With acceptance, you gain:

- Peace. The internal battle ends. All that resisting and worry takes its toll.
- Plan. You can now plan your days.
- Preparation. You can now prepare for what's to come. You'll be ready.
- Priorities. You now wisely choose how to spend your time.
- Perspective. You no longer take it personally. You move from asking "Why me?" to "Okay, it's me. What's my next step?"
- Prosperity. You have energy, time, resources and love.

Most important, with acceptance, you gain today. Your life is in the moments of today. With acceptance, you live in today, for today.

Resilience: Bounce Back from Bad Days

Sarah has had a rough day, an even rougher one than yesterday and she thought a day couldn't get worse than that one.

Her father has been with her for three years. He's living on borrowed time. At 88-years-old he's suffered three strokes and was recently diagnosed with terminal colon cancer. She knows that he won't be with her for much longer and tries to draw strength from that. She can be with him now, she thinks, because this is the last time they will be together.

If only her sister would help her more! Her sister seems to be someone new, someone she's never met before. Her sister used to be such a caring person, always available to lend a helping hand, to listen with an open heart. But, these last few weeks... Her sister can only be described as, well, awful.

Yesterday, her husband was rushed to the emergency room from work because of a slight heart attack. Scared them both to death. He's home now and expected to recover, as long as he makes changes in his lifestyle. On Tuesday, he was a strong, virile man. Today, two days later, he's a baby who can't heat up his own soup.

How in the world will Sarah make it through these next few weeks, with her husband home recovering from a heart attack and her father in the spare bedroom dying of cancer and her sister, well, angry at the world?

Sarah stares at the television, at her favorite TV show, which usually cheers her up. She's too spent to cry. How am I going to do this? How am I going to survive this?

Resilience is a caregiver's secret weapon. It's what will get Sarah up the next day. It's what will keep her going. Every family caregiver knows the feeling of those low points. We also know that we somehow wake up the next day, get out of bed, and face it again. We don't know any other way.

Staying resilient also means staying healthy. And, when you're a family caregiver, your mental and physical wellness may sometimes be jeopardized. If you don't feel good about one area of your life (especially an area such as caregiving), how you feel about the remaining areas (your job, your marriage, your children, your friendships) may be at risk. Keeping your caregiving role in check is imperative so that when life's darts get thrown, you're in shape to handle the hits.

Some reminders to maintain your wellness as a family caregiver:

1. Let in. You're probably the best caregiver in your family but you're not the only one. Your spouse can read to your caree on a Saturday afternoon so you can get out with friends. Your siblings can provide financial support so you can hire home health aides and give yourself a regular break from laundry, cooking and cleaning. Your adult children can spend an evening with your caree so you can enjoy dinner and a show. Your out-of-town relatives can telephone your caree regularly so you're not the only one providing social interaction with your caree. And, ask for help rather than wait for others to offer. You'll wait forever.

2. Define your caregiving role, don't let it define you. Enjoy activities on a regular basis that remind you of you--your interests, your ideas, your opinions and your values. Make adjustments in your caregiving duties that allow time for those activities to happen on a daily, weekly, semi-monthly basis, whatever you can manage.

3. Make sure caregiving in some way affects your life in a positive way. Reap some benefits, rather than just making sacrifices. Has caregiving taught you about the positive power of giving? Have you gained an understanding about your caree that you never had before? Have you learned about patience and virtue? Have you learned how strong and successful you can be no matter the obstacles or stresses?

4. Seek a support system and nourish it. Does a relative, friend or caregiving acquaintance support and validate your efforts? Everyone needs an empathetic ear and sympathetic shoulder, especially family caregivers. In turn, be supportive to other family caregivers. Our daily chats at CareGiving.com offer both support and comfort. In addition, our family caregivers who blog on CareGiving.com tell us the process of writing and releasing their worries and anxieties is very cathartic. You can start your own blog on a variety of websites, including CareGiving.com.

5. Make sure your motivation as a caregiver is honest and healthy. For instance, in your caregiving role, are you hoping to right the wrongs of past relationships? Is that realistic? And, most important, is that healthy? Or, are you a caregiver because you understand and appreciate its importance to you and your family? Keep on top of your motivation; if you find yourself slipping into the motivating ways of a martyr, pull up and re-examine your role. What's best for you, your caree, your family? Counselors and life coaches can be a resource for you as you work to stay in a healthy place.

6. Remain realistic. Continue to educate yourself about your caree's illness or disease. Learn how to handle difficult behavior, provide hands-on care and administer treatments. Ask your caree's physician, your home care workers and organizations such as the Alzheimer's Association for suggestions and information to make you a well-informed, trained family caregiver. Knowledge can help minimize your frustration and uncertainty.

Resilience holds its power. The better you get at bouncing back, the easier it will be to recover from caregiving's bad days.

Quiz: How Well Do You Bounce Back?

How well do you recover from your day-to-day challenges as a family caregiver? Take our quick test to find out.

A. Your sister-in-law pops in for another visit, unannounced, of course. And, of course, it's on your worst day. You're still in your pajamas (splattered with oatmeal, smelling of, well, just smelling), your husband is angry and defiant (I won't go to adult day care today!) and your dog is throwing up.

"I thought I'd drop off a plant for Frank on my way to work," she says. Before you can say another word, she's in your house and staring at her brother and then lashing out at you, "What have you done to him?"

You:

1. Let her have it, venting all the frustrations and anger you've held in for the past five years.

2. Take a deep breath and explain, "We're having a bad day. But, I'm so glad you're here. I'd love your help. I'll just run upstairs and take a quick shower while you visit with Frank." Before you've finished your sentence, you're calling to her from the upstairs bathroom. You don't give her a chance to refuse. You amaze yourself at your ability to bound up the stairs in seconds. You can't remember the last time you moved so fast.

3. You sit on the couch and cry. This is too hard!

B. Your mother calls you, for the 20th time, at work to let you know that she can't find her purse. Yesterday, she called you, at work, 25 times to let you know she had missed her dental appointment. You're going to lose your job if this keeps up.

You:

1. Quit your job, even though your lack of income jeopardizes your future.

2. Call your local Area Agency on Agency, local chapter of the Alzheimer's Association, your church. There's got to be a solution to this and you're going to find it.

3. Put your phone on "Do Not Disturb."

C. The home health aide is late. Again. You've spoken to her about how important her promptness is to you. But, she seems to go by a different clock than you.

You:

1. Tell the aide you've changed her start time to 9:30 a.m. You'd like her at your house at 10 a.m. You know she'll be on time now. That'll teach her!

2. Call her supervisor and explain the situation. What suggestions can she offer to solve the problem?

3. Do nothing. What can you do? It's hard to find good help.

D. The nursing home staff promised to keep track of your mother's laundry. But yet another visit uncovers yet another problem–no matching socks. Your mother is wearing a pink sock and a yellow sock neither of which match her favorite purple housecoat. This makes you crazy.

You:

1. March to the administrator's office, bursting into a closed-door meeting. You demand to know, "Why am I paying you $7,000 a month to dress my mother like a clown?"

2. Decide to do your mother's laundry. Actually, you'll ask your granddaughters to help.

3. Spend the rest of the visit looking for that one pink sock and that one yellow sock. Somebody's got to be wearing them!

What's your score?

Mostly 2's: You're in good shape! You face everyday challenges well, compromising when necessary, but never giving up that solutions exist. You're resilient!

Mostly 3's: You have good intentions, which will help you on your way to being resilient. You struggle to find the positives in situations which can lead to effective solutions. Rather than giving up, work on strengthening your emotional and physical well-being.

Mostly 1's: You're a walking time bomb! Your anger and mistrust seem to get the best of you and every challenging situation you encounter. Practice keeping your patience by thinking of creative and unusual solutions and viewing a situation from all sides. Sometimes, all is not what it seems.

Ask Denise: Is the Guilt About Esteem?

Dear Denise,

I schedule time away from my caree, but feel guilty for doing so even though I know I want and need the time away.

Is feeling guilty related to self-esteem?

Hello,

What a great question.

The short answer is Yes.

Let's break it down.

Here's the good about your guilt. Your ability to feel guilty shows your great capacity to feel for another. You can appreciate another's pain or sadness or loneliness, you can put yourself in another's shoes. Your caring nature is a good virtue.

It can become a problem, though, if you seem to care more for others than you do for yourself or if your guilt seems to get in the way of you living your life.

Here's the definition of guilt:
1. the fact or state of having committed an offense, crime, violation, or wrong, esp. against moral or penal law; culpability: He admitted his guilt.
2. a feeling of responsibility or remorse for some offense, crime, wrong, etc., whether real or imagined.
3. conduct involving the commission of such crimes, wrongs, etc.: to live a life of guilt.

Consider the second definition: A feeling of responsibility or remorse for some offense, crime, wrong, etc., whether real or imagined.

Let's say you're taking a break you want to take*, you've put back-up care in place, you've provided solutions to all anticipated problems, and you've created a phone tree of persons who can be contacted in case of an emergency.

When you leave, you still feel guilty. What offense could you have committed?

It could be you feel guilty because you will enjoy a life outside of caregiving when your caree cannot really enjoy a life outside of a disease process (or frailty or permanent injury). Your offense, truly, may be that you are healthy enough to enjoy an activity, a vacation, an experience.

Is that really an offense worthy of that awful feeling of guilt?

What could keep you in a place where thoughts such as "I don't deserve to have this time away because I don't deserve to have health" live? Yep, a lack of confidence. When a caree says, "I don't know how you can feel good about leaving me here while you traipse around the city," you'll think, "Oh, he's right. I don't deserve this time away."

Seems kinda nutty, doesn't it?

If you come from a place of confidence, you may be able to say, "I am taking this break because I deserve time for just me. I work hard and I deserve a break." When your caree says, "A good daughter would stay here with her mother in her time of need," you can say, "I am a good daughter. I'll be back tonight about 10 p.m. I'll stop by your room to say 'Good Night'."

When our self-esteem takes a dip, we leave more room for others to fill it with their own baggage. When we're not feeling good about ourselves, we open the door for others to plunk down their own luggage of self-doubt in our room. Their own dirty laundry—insecurities and lack of confidence—spills over and adds to our own.

Even worse, when we're low, we often allow others to dictate how we feel.

When we're full, we own our own emotions.

Believe in your own goodness. Believe that you make good decisions about your own needs and wants. It's okay if others can't be happy for you or support you. That's their choice. You choose otherwise.

*Please note that you'll have times during your caregiving experience when others will encourage you to take a break and you know it's not the time to take a break. In this article, we're only referring to the times you've made plans to take a break and it's a break you really want.

Ask Denise: How Do I Leave Without Guilt?

Dear Denise,

I have taken care of my mom and dad for the past almost 10 years (my dad died a year ago) and now I must relinquish that responsibility due to her inability to stay alone while I work. At her last hospitalization, she was diagnosed with an aggressive lymphoma for which, due to her heart health, aggressive treatment can not be done. I have huge guilt feelings about placement in nursing home but at the same time I know she is being well cared for. How do you walk away without the guilt when she appears fine and is extremely angry with me about where she is?

Hi,

What a rough road for you and your mom this last year. While grieving for your dad, you find out really upsetting news about your mom. And, then, because of this news, you have to make a really difficult decision. It would be nice if you could get a break with some good news.

A few thoughts for you:

It's okay that your mom is angry. It may seem she's angry with you but she's much angrier at her disease, her circumstances, her twist of fate. But, how can you be mad at something you can't see or hear or touch? It's much easier to be angry at you because you're a tangible target.

When she expresses her anger, acknowledge and empathize, but don't take it on as your own. You can say, "I understand how difficult this situation is, Mom. Given all the losses you've experienced this year, it's understandable that you feel so angry." Then, give her a few moments to vent.

After a few minutes, tell her, "I wish it were different, too. I know you're doing your best to adjust. I'm so grateful for every minute we have together. Let's talk about this weekend. How do you want to spend Saturday?"

Often when we're angry we just want someone to tell us that, given all that's happened, we deserve to feel angry. If someone tries to minimize or diminish our anger, it just adds more fuel to the anger fire.

When you leave her, simply say, "I love you, Mom. I'll call you tomorrow and see you tomorrow night (or whatever your calling/visiting schedule will be). Thank you for all you do for me."

I think it's hard to leave your mom without feeling any emotion. When you leave, acknowledge to yourself that you leave with sadness. It is such a sad situation! Give yourself time to feel that sadness and find a way to let it out. Ask the nursing home social worker if the facility has a support group for family members. Talk to family members and friends. Write about it in a journal.

Do you best to fight the guilt. If she lived with you, you would feel guilty for leaving to go to work. If she lived in her own apartment, you would feel guilty that she lived on her own and not with you. There's so much to feel guilty about which is why I hope you'll let yourself off the hook.

10 Ways to Get Even With the No-Help Sibling

In August 2015, my oldest sibling removed herself from helping our parents. She no longer participates and no longer sees myself, my siblings or my parents.

She stopped helping because she really got angry with me and one of my brothers. She's mad because we expressed concerns over a decision she made about our mother's care, which became a nightmare of a situation I ultimately had to resolve. I'm not sure why being angry with me means she must sever her ties with my parents. But that's how it's been.

It's so easy for one year to stretch into another and another. I feel the caregiving fate is sealed for ourselves and for her. I just can't imagine her positioning herself to be back in the fold to participate in our family, much less help our parents. I can't even imagine her calling my parents or visiting my parents or joining us in a family celebration. Visiting my parents does not present a hardship for her as she lives five minutes from them and she works out of her home. Yet, she drives by their apartment without a call or a visit. My younger sister and I discuss whether we will be invited to her family's celebrations, like when one of her daughters marries. I hope so but I'm just not sure.

Once in a while--not often--I do get caught up in the idea of revenge. Once I even said to my parents, "Are you sure you want her to inherent that money you worked so hard to earn?" My parents, wisely, ignored my idea. I recently had the thought that I should write my name on a piece of tape that I attach to the bottom of my parents' possessions so she doesn't get what I believe I deserve. I stared down that temptation, though. Who am I to sit and judge the distribution of my parents' salt and pepper shakers?

So, I guess I'll get even this way:

1. I'll love her children. Our fracture has affected my relationship with my nieces because we just don't see them as often. I'm going to change that, though, and make a much better effort about keeping in touch and getting together (if they want).

2. I'm going to sleep well tonight. I'm not perfect. I'm impatience and often harsh with my words. I am, however, still fully present with and in our parents' care.

3. I'm going to continue to carefully craft the legacy I leave to the next generation. I hope my actions will create a legacy I will feel proud to leave behind. I often think about the legacy Sibling leaves for her children and with us. I wonder how that legacy will take shape when Sibling needs help. Will our memories of Sibling be the memories she really wants us to keep?

4. I will treasure the relationships I have with my three other siblings. They are so kind and compassionate and supportive. I want to take care of those relationships because they mean so much to me.

5. I will let go of who I think she should be because that's not possible for her. I'll let go so when I see her next, which could be at a parent's funeral, I will be gracious.

6. I will learn from this situation because I truly understand how important it is to admit when I'm wrong and then move on. Because everyone else has. When I don't, I just turn one wrong into a road built from a ton of wrongs that leads to bitterness. Everyone else will wonder what in the world has gotten into me.

7. I will love her, no matter what, even though I hate how much pain she causes our parents.

8. I will be sure to absorb and document the stories my parents tell me about their childhoods, their marriage and our childhoods.

9. I will choose kindness as often and as much as I can. Kindness keeps life sweet.

10. I will put a priority on peace because turmoil simply turns a day into a nightmare. When peace remains my top concern, I listen when others tell me I'm wrong. I don't start a war just to prove they're wrong.

The best revenge? Knowing I stayed because I know how easy it is to just leave. Or, maybe I now see how easy it is to leave and hard it is to live with yourself once you do leave. Sometimes our choices become the cement that hardens our heart so much that even a summer heat wave can't melt them. I would rather choose to stay warm to life regardless of the season.

"A day without laughter is a day wasted." ~ Charlie Chaplin

Stage IV:
The Pragmatic Caregiver

I am still caring for a family member or friend.

Who are you?

You've been through it all: hospital admission and discharges; short-term rehab stays in nursing homes; a vast array of community services. You've been through the health care system long enough to know that you know your caree's needs best.

Because you've overcome so much, you now get it. It could be that you get what letting go means. It could be that you get it's not your responsibility to do it all and to be everything to everyone. It could be that you get the importance of using time wisely. It could be that you get that when someone shows you the first time who they are, you believe them. (Perspective courtesy of Maya Angelou.) You've earned the wisdom you now wear.

You understand that you are not meant to be superhuman for yourself, for your caree, for your family, in your career. Because you embrace your humanity, you put the hamster wheel in the closet. You no longer chase perfectionism and instead welcome your best, whatever that may be, in any given moment.

You also get the importance of a good laugh. Some family members and health care professionals may wonder about your ability to find humor in situations they find odd. You have a very practical, very realistic approach toward your caregiving role and your sense of humor has been a critical tool for your survival. Without your sense of humor, you would have given up a long time ago.

Your Keyword: Welcome

--Welcome the joys of your connections with your caree and with others.
--Welcome forgiveness of yourself, of your caree, of other family members and friends.
--Welcome shared activities, even simple ones like laughing together.
--Welcome possibilities for your future.
--Welcome what is and what will be.

Your Challenge

To gain a greater understanding of yourself and your caree.

Your Purpose

To gain a better understanding of yourself and your caree. You've settled into your role and your routine; now is your opportunity to step back and reflect. The first three stages laid the groundwork for this stage, your period of personal growth.

Judy and Frank

Frank insists that he is continent, that he can make it to the bathroom when he needs to. Judy knows better, as she continually scrubs and cleans soaked linens, clothes, furniture and carpeting. Judy watches with a steady gaze as visiting nurse after visiting nurse insist that Frank wear adult disposable briefs. Then, after they leave, she watches Frank curse the nurse and the briefs, throwing the new box of 32 briefs brought by the nurse against the wall. As a monument to Frank's stubbornness, Judy stacks the dented boxes on top of each other on the back porch. Her children refuse to use the back door and pass the pyramid of briefs, a display they find to be distasteful. Judy, when she needs a good laugh, stands in the middle of the back porch.

Abigail and Andy

Over time, Andy finds he enjoys his mother's phone calls and her requests for the time, the names of her friends, the departure of the facility van for the shopping mall. When the calls first became intense, Andy resented the infringement on his time, as well as the need for him to keep in touch with the facility's social worker. Now he realizes his phone calls with his mother are a major reason why Abigail has been able to remain in her retirement community.

When the social worker calls with updates which are never good, Andy finds himself asking the social worker: Did my mother kill anyone today? Did my mother steal anyone's dinner roll off their plate? Did my mother pick a fight with anyone today? The social worker repeatedly insists she finds these questions offensive, but for Andy, these questions encourage a good laugh, and remind him it's not the end of the world.

In his email updates to his siblings, Andy includes more reflections on his role, which he now sees as critical to his mother's life. He shares with his siblings without feeling any pain toward them. Instead, he feels grateful that he has done all he has.

As a "pragmatic caregiver," what can you do?

1. Work on finding joy during your connections with your caree.
The biggest joy-killer can be your hands-on duties like bathing, dressing and incontinence care. But these duties bring you together, this is your time together. Add some fun to your hands-on care by singing songs, telling jokes and sharing goals and dreams.

A Stumble: You care for your mother-in-law and, quite honestly, you don't like her. She doesn't like you. At all. Because of your shared dislike, you toss aside the possibility that you might find joy in the relationship.

A Steady: You do have more in common than your shared dislike because you both love the same man. Use this as a bridge to gain a more positive perspective toward your mother-in-law.

2. Work on forgiving.
Resentment toward past wrong and injustices will make your present caregiving role very difficult. Let go of what was and concentrate on making what is healthy and productive. Forgiving others, including your caree, your family members, the health care system and your faith, is one of the best ways you take care of yourself.

3. Develop a habit of enjoying shared activities.
Develop a routine of time shared as husband-wife, mother-daughter, father-son rather than as just caregiver and caree. Releasing the roles of family caregiver and caree allows you to enjoy each other.

4. Begin to think about your future.
What's your dream? How can put plans in place to create it? If appropriate, how can your caree be a part of your vision?

5. Discover a different definition of achievement.
How can you redefine success to reflect who you are now? What's a new commitment you can make to open up possibilities and opportunities?

6. An apple a day…
What's your apple in this stage? What helps you to feel good on a daily basis? You may feel like trying something new. That's good! You can never have too many apples.

The Pragmatic Caregiver
Your Reflections

In this stage, what are your goals?
—For your caree?

—For you?

—For your family?

How will you achieve these goals?

Who can help you achieve these goals?

What do you most love/respect about your caree?

What do you miss about your caree?

How can recreate some of the good times you shared?

The Pragmatic Caregiver
Your Resource Library

Your Greatest Skill: You Know How

I regularly present my workshop, Healing the Family Rift, to groups of social workers and family caregivers. (You can watch the free webinar on CareGiving.com). During the presentation, the attendees will share their stories of rifts that leave them wounded. For the family caregivers in the audience, the wounds come because other family members just won't help.

During one particular presentation, Anne, who cares for her mom and also cared for dad, shared her story. She's one of six siblings but the only adult child who helps. She couldn't understand how her siblings could not help their mother, now in her 90s and suffering from dementia. "She has Alzheimer's," Anne said, "and she's exceptional."

I later asked Anne to share a little more about one of the siblings who doesn't help. Anne told the audience about her younger sister, who told Anne, "I want to keep my life as it is. Helping Mom will complicate it." Anne's youngest sister travels regularly to wonderful places like Dubai. Her sister gives to herself. Anne gives to their mother.

As Anne shared about her sister, members of the audience chimed in with their thoughts. "She must just not know how," someone suggested.

Anne shared more of the story. When their father was dying, Anne said, it was really hard. She told her sister just how hard it was.

Ah, I said. It's hard to be there and yet you still did it.

It's hard for your sister, I added. She can't figure out a way to be there. Just think how hard it is to know that and even harder it must be to admit it to someone who knows how.

So, she travels. Really, she runs.

When family caregivers share stories of siblings who can't, I think of an email I received several years ago. A sister, caring for her mother, wrote to me about her brother. He stopped by like clockwork at the same time on the same day every week to see his sister and mother, who resided in an upstairs bedroom in his sister's house. When the brother made his visit, he stood in the hallway of this sister's house, never going further into the home, never actually seeing his mother.

This made his sister crazy. What is wrong with him, she said, that he can't come and visit with me and sit with his mother?

I wrote her back with the following suggestion. "The next time your brother arrives, give him a hug and tell him, 'I'm so glad you are here.' Then, take his hand and walk him up the stairs and into your mom's room. Sit with him as he sits with your mom. Talk to your mom and help him do the same. He wants to be there for both of you. He just doesn't know how."

Rosyln Carter speaks of four kinds of people in the world: Those who have been caregivers, those who are currently caregivers, those who will be caregivers and those who will need caregivers.

I wonder, though, if it's more like two kinds of people: Those who know how and those who need us to show them how.

You know how because you stay when you'd like to run. You stay when you think, "This is so awful. I'm not sure I can do this." You get up every day to begin again, to face the difficulties that come with life's hard time.

And, interestingly enough, you show them how by doing what you do every day. Just doing it. Once in awhile you can show them by telling them, "I understand that this is hard. I have days when I doubt myself. I have moments when I question whether or not I'm doing what's right, what's best. When it gets that hard, I talk it out, I take a moment to breathe and I say a prayer."

You show them how to manage those doubts and worries we all experience. When we know how to face our own demons, we know how to stay.

My presentation ended with thoughts on how to move past the anger, resentment and bitterness toward those family members who don't help. Anne told us that she wants to heal, that she has packages to mail to siblings in hopes her bitterness will fade when the boxes begin their journey.

I'm reminded of a story shared with me by a former family caregiver ten years after her experience ended. Her siblings were minimally involved in helping her care for their mother. The family caregiver was with her mother as her mother died, an experience that still moves her when she speaks about it. After her mom died, she called her siblings to let know them their mother had died and to describe her mother's final moments. After hearing about these final moments, her sister said, "I should have been there."

The family caregiver lives in peace knowing she was there. The sister lives with regrets knowing she should have been there.

We could judge those who don't know how. Sometimes, the judging does feel good. In the end, though, we don't have to judge because those who don't know how will be their own toughest judges. Think of Anne's sister. When her mother dies, will she view her trips to those exotic places with fondness? Or, will they be viewed with shame? The plane she took never took her to where she really wanted to be—with her mom. She just didn't know how to get on the right plane. Anne will be able to live with herself when caregiving is over. How will her sister?

I spoke with Anne after the presentation. She was on her way to mail her gifts. Because she knows how. Just like you.

At Some Point, Create a Plan to Avoid Hospitalizations

My father's best friend, Richard, died a few years ago. My parents were on vacation when Richard died so Richard's daughter reached out to me. During our phone conversation, I asked about her father's last weeks.

They were chaotic.

Richard fell at home. A son found his father after his father had been laying on the floor for a few hours. They brought him to the emergency room, where he waited for hours to be admitted. Once admitted, he endured more tests to see how far his bone cancer had spread. After an x-ray, the technician actually dropped a piece of equipment on Richard's foot. "What are you trying to do, kill me?" exclaimed a typically mild-mannered Richard.

During most of your caregiving experience, hospitalizations are part of treatment. In the hospital, your caree receives the diagnosis, treatments and sometimes a cure, even if only a temporary one. A hospitalization is necessary because it has what you don't have at home to get your caree better.

At some point, though, you may want to create a plan to avoid the hospitalizations. I regularly mention a podcast I did a few years ago with Dr. Maison ("Making the Most of End-Of-Life*) during which he offered a really helpful perspective.

As we seek more and more medical attention for our carees, take advantage of the opportunity to talk to health care professionals about the future. For instance, during a re-hospitalization for a similar reason, on the last hospital day, begin the conversation with your caree's physician by asking questions. What options do we have other than another hospitalization? Can we prevent another hospitalization? If we can't, what other options do we have? What kind of improvement in my caree's condition can we expect? How can I best keep my caree comfortable?

I think of my father's friend, Richard, who spent some of his last days in the hospital. The hospitals days were traumatic and upsetting for Richard and his family. What if they had created a plan to avoid the hospital?

What if they asked the hospice staff about possible falls and how to prevent a trip to the hospital? Or, better yet, what if the hospice staff spoke with Richard and his family about the possibility of falls and asked, "How would you like to manage a fall? We can create a plan to keep you at home, Richard." When the fall happened, the family could have called the hospice nurse on staff, who could have visited Richard at home, assessed the situation and then spoken with the doctor to create a treatment plan to keep Richard comfortable.

One of my coaching clients cared for her mom at home. On a Tuesday morning, my client's mom fell and perhaps broke her ankle. My client called the hospice nurse who ensured her mom stayed home, comfortable and out of pain. My client's mom died on Sunday.

My client struggled with the fall. "What could I have done differently?" she asked. "How could I let that happen?" The reality is that falls happen. The reality was that her mom was entering her last days. The fall didn't cause her mom's death. Rather, her mom's body began shutting down and then the fall happened.

The most important reality is that her mom died at home--the long-term goal my client held--rather than in the hospital.

End of life can mean more falls and more frequent infections. It's important to talk about how to manage when the falls and infections happen. At the beginning of caregiving, situations like falls and infections mean a trip to the hospital. At the end of life, perhaps falls and infections can be best managed at home, where there is no waiting room full of really sick people, there is no clumsy technician, there is no stranger who is now a roommate, there is no middle-of-the-night poking and probing.

At home, we can provide comfort and familiar and calm. When days are numbered, you can never have too much comfort, familiar and calm.

* You can listen to the podcast here:
caregiving.com/2010/01/making-the-most-of-end-of-life/

"Perhaps they are not stars, but rather openings in heaven where the love of our lost ones pours through and shines down upon us to let us know they are happy."
~ Eskimo Proverb

Stage V:
The Transitioning Caregiver

My role is changing.

Who are you?
You've been caring for a period of time and now can sense the end.

Your Keyword: Allow
--Allow time to mourn and grieve.
--Allow remembrances to remain.
--Allow reflections of your experiences.

Your Challenge
To let go of the fear of the end, to understand that reaching the end isn't about your failure but about the natural cycle of life. Now, you'll move from the "doing" of caregiving to focus on the "being." You're used to doing and going. It's time now to make being with your caree the priority.

During caregiving, you've been in a battle. Most recently, you've been fighting death hoping to keep death's visit to your caree at bay.

You can end the fight because you've won the battle. You've done enough and are enough. You've long worried that a caree's death could somehow be your fault. You can now know that you've given your caree a life for as long as your caree's life could continue. You no longer have to try everything and do whatever is possible. You understand that over-doing now could create more discomfort and pain for your caree. When you end your internal battle, you can be fully present with your caree. Your peaceful presence is your power.

Your Purpose
To walk with your caree during his last months and weeks, implementing his or her decisions about end-of-life care that you both discussed during Stage I (or as soon as you could). You can focus on loving and feeling good about the shared journey. As you both feel the journey end, this is also a time to mourn and grief. You also will begin to question and worry about your life's next chapter.

Judy and Frank
Caring for Frank at home became an exhausting task for Judy. She lost the fight against bed sores several times, not out of neglect but just because

the enormity of the task was too much for one person. The home health aides helped but they weren't there at night to change and turn Frank. Besides, they only helped six hours a week. Judy didn't sleep well at night and was just too exhausted to do much of anything, including enjoy her Sunday morning excursion to church and lunch, a ritual she once never missed.

At her children's insistence, she visits nursing homes near her home and finds one that she can afford and that she feels can provide the care Frank needs. Frank is admitted and now Judy struggles to find a new daily routine.

Andy and Abigail

Abigail's condition has worsened and a CAT scan reveals a brain tumor and a terminal diagnosis. It seems that overnight Abigail has become a very confused, very fragile and very unhealthy 86-year-old woman. Rather than admit his mother to a nursing home in Brooklyn, Andy moves his mother to his home in Denver. He takes a leave from his company, opting to take advantage of the Family Medical Leave Act.

With the assistance of a hospice organization, Andy cares for his mother in his home until her death. His siblings are with their mother when she dies, a blessing Andy relishes. He knows how important their visit was to their mother.

Just weeks after his mother's death, Andy returns to work, but finds "transitioning back into the real world" very difficult. His concerns for his mother had engulfed him for more than three years. He's having difficulty "turning off" his caregiving role. Who am I, he wonders.

As a "transitioning caregiver," what can you do?

1. Use your best judgment as to when you take breaks.
You now have a limited amount of time to spend with your caree. Trust your gut and spend as much time as feels right for you. When others encourage you to take a break and you know it's not the right time, let them know, "Time with my caree is my priority. I appreciate your concern. I'm okay."

2. Know that being with your careee is how you do for your caree.
You've done so much for your caree. Because of all you did, your caree has seemingly lived nine lives. You'll be tempted to continue doing at the same pace. You'll continue doing, especially ensuring your caree receives the best quality care, but with a different purpose. In this stage, being is as

important as doing. Know that being, like simply sitting and holding hands, also can be the best way to do for your caree. You've both earned this time to be just where you are in the journey.

3. Consider hospice before you think it's time.
If you contact hospice too soon, you've just bought yourself some time. If you contact hospice too late, then you've missed out on support and comfort for your caree, your family and yourself. As soon as you begin to wonder about hospice, make a phone call to a hospice organization to learn about the right time for its services. Hospice provides services regardless of where your caree lives—your home, her home or the nursing home.

4. When your caree speaks of death, continue the conversation.
Your caree may want to talk about death. You may be tempted to stop the conversations, believing a discussion about death is like giving up. When your caree brings up death, be open to listening and talking. Ask questions like "What do you think about dying?" and "What do you fear about death?" Share your own feelings including ones like "I'm going to miss you." As difficult as these discussions may be now, you will find comfort in them later.

5. The release of fear, the ability to "be", can add a spiritual component to your tasks.
Your caregiving tasks may take on greater importance to you, as you see yourself caring for your caree who now exists in a holding pattern between life and death. You may see these duties—the personal care, the feeding, the bathing—as readying your caree for the final journey. You can look at your hands as doing God's work here on earth. You will see the sacredness in your days.

6. Let others in.
Those family members and friends who disappeared may now reappear, anxious to visit your caree. The temptation may be to make these visits difficult for those family members and friends, believing they haven't earned the right to be involved now. Let go of that temptation and let the visits happen. Ask the hospice staff for help managing the visits if you worry that the dysfunction may become a distraction. Be at peace, like Andy, because you have no regrets. When you avoid judging, you keep your inner peace.

7. Take a break. Or don't. You decide.
When time becomes limited with your caree, you may spend more and more time with your caree which may prompt others to encourage you to take a break. That suggestion may be a helpful reminder or a horrible idea. You choose when and if the time is right for the break.

8. Allow yourself time to mourn and grief.
Both Judy and Andy are experiencing tremendous losses. For Judy, this may be a time of greater mourning than when her husband dies.

A Stumble: You may find that your current support group no longer meets your needs. You just seem to be on a different wave length than the other caregivers.

A Steady: Find a bereavement or grief support group. Your local hospice agency can be instrumental in helping you understand and deal with your grief. You may find that your period of mourning lasts a long time, maybe your lifetime. That's normal as long as, at some point, you're able to move on with your life. It's not normal if you feel paralyzed. A professional counselor may be able to help you transition into a new chapter of your life.

9. Create Your Replacement Therapy.
After caregiving ends, you're left with too much time and feel like you have too little to do. Donna Webb, who cared for her mom and blogged on CareGiving.com, created the idea of Replacement Therapy, replacing the time spent on a caregiving task with another task.
   You can do that, too. Here's how:

- Write down the caregiving schedule, including times and tasks.
- Once you have your list, write what you enjoyed about each task.
- Use this list of enjoyments to begin to recreate your day. Replace the caregiving activity with an activity that creates a similar experience or emotion or enjoyment for you. Maybe during the time when you fed your caree, you now bake or document your caree's favorite recipes. Perhaps during the time when you provided personal care, you now create with your hands.
- Consider building in some quiet time. During the quiet time, consider how you will use free time when you have it. How will you bring your caregiving knowledge to the community? Who will

you be and what will you do in your future? What would your caree wish for you during this next stage of life?
- Finally, this transitioning will be bumpy. Feel the bumps and take time to readjust. The bumps can be a great guide.

10. Remember your caree.
You don't have to give away clothes or remove pictures until you want to. When family and friends seem hesitant to talk about your caree because they worry they will upset you, assure them that sharing memories and stories brings you comfort.

A Stumble: Your daughter tells you that your husband's clothes, which still hang in your closet, should be given away, that it's unhealthy to keep his clothes.

A Steady: Consider your daughter's comments. Are you ready to give away his clothes? If not, can you pinpoint what's holding you back? What's a fear, worry, or a concern? What's best for you?

11. Reflect back on your caregiving responsibilities and decisions with pride.
Find comfort in knowing that you did the best you could. When your thoughts try to trick you into believing you could have done more, reframe those thoughts into knowing you did all you could with the information, resources, support and energy you had. Your caree knows this, too, and sends you messages of deep gratitude.

12. Be curious about what's next for you.
You may feel disconnected to who you were and unsure of who you are. Rather than rush into decisions, simply be curious about what's possible. Accept that you will have moments of discomfort and confusion. You will find your way.

13. Review your journal.
How are you different and better today than you were on the day you first started writing in your journal? How will you use this experience to enhance your future?

14. Learn about your transition to your next chapter.
My book, *After Caregiving Ends, A Guide to Beginning Again,* offers insights

as you step into what's next. You also can enroll in our virtual six-week course, "Beginning Again After Caregiving Ends" on CareGiving.com. For details, visit www.caregiving.com/courses.

15. An apple a day...
What's your apple in this stage? You may feel that an apple in this stage is unnecessary. Take an apple. It's what keeps you feeling like you.

The Transitioning Caregiver
Your Reflections

In this stage, what are your goals?
—For your caree?

—For you?

—For your family?

How will you achieve these goals?

Who can help you achieve these goals?

What are you most proud of as a family caregiver?

Which memories of your caree are most comforting to you?

The Transitioning Caregiver
Your Resource Library

Ask Denise: What Do I Do? He Didn't Help

Dear Denise,

First, I have to tell you what a wonderful community you have on caregiving.com. Thank you for your work at creating and maintaining such a supportive environment.

I don't know what "answer" I'm looking for but know you will have an answer that will be perfect for me. My situation is that I care for a relative and we are a very small family. I handle the caregiving duties and, although my sibling generously helps financially, he is very hands off. (To be fair, he lives over an hour away.) I have always been positive I could count on him if I ever needed him.

Recently, my caree had a severe decline in health and it was a scary situation. I called my sibling and asked he visit my caree. He told me he was very busy (who isn't?). I don't do this very often (this was the only time this year and probably longer than that), but I pushed and made it clear he needed to visit. He did but it was obvious he wasn't happy about it.

Shortly after that visit, I visited him at his house with my caree. My sister-in-law "talked" with me about how I shouldn't have pushed, I am not my sibling's "mom" and that I was completely wrong to insist my caree be visited by this sibling. Both she and my sibling made comments to the effect that the caree "wasn't dying." I was very hurt since I asked him to visit not just as support for my caree but for me too (maybe even more for me).

My relationship with my sibling has always been solid. I feel a paradigm shift here and I'm not liking it. I am inclined to continue to update my sibling on my caree's condition but not insist on visits--even rarely. I think I need to accept my sibling's part of caregiving is strictly financial and mine is hands-on. Is this the right approach? Was I expecting too much to insist on the visit?

Signed, Anti-Change

Hi A-C,

I'm so glad you find the website helpful.

You and your brother obviously share a special bond, which is why you looked to him during a very frightening time. I think our relationships with our siblings are so important to us because siblings are the ones in our life who share our personal history. They know—we don't have to explain anything.

What's interesting to me is our shared history doesn't mean we share the same priorities or values or perspectives. This can be sooo frustrating and, often, very painful.

I found that making requests means I have to let go of what I expect others to do as a result of my request. My expectation for myself is that I make a clear request by asking for what I need and explaining why it's important to me.

Here's the trick. Once I make the request, I let go of the outcome. I speak up, explain what I need and why it's important to me. That's all I can do. I have to leave the outcome (what others decide about my request) up to them. And, I have to trust that the decision they make is right for them.

Which of course leads to the next tricky part. A decision that's right for them may not be right for me. I have to accept that.

When something like the decline happens again, update your brother. Let him know you'd love a visit if he can. Then let him know how grateful you are for him. This sounds nutty but I find it works. You also could ask, "How often would you like me to update you on this situation?" When he tells you, you both understand how to go forward.

Then, move to what you need--love and support from others in your life. Lean on those who can be the comforting presence for you during those scary and upsetting times. You also could look to build support now for any future upsets. Ask others now if they could be available to support you in another crisis with phone calls, email messages and, if possible, visits.

You mention that you're feeling a shift in your relationship with your brother. I wonder if you could look at the shift as one in perspectives, but not one in how you both feel about each other. Certainly, a shift has taken place; you look at your brother differently now, at least temporarily. Feel the disappointment and hurt. When you can, reset your expectations and then move into accepting him and his decisions. Look at what happened as communication about boundaries; your brother and sister-in-law have set a boundary. That's okay. Keep the love in your heart for him (and her). There's room in your life for him to make different decisions and have other priorities and for you to continue to love him. Know he will always love you. Let this be a bump, rather than a fork, in the road.

Finally, I also wonder if it feels like you did something wrong. Certainly your sister-in-law chiding you couldn't feel good. It's always right to express what you need. Let go of any regrets you may have over what happened. You did what felt right to you during a really stressful time. You can never go wrong doing that.

The Saddest Switch: From Searching for a Cure to Providing Comfort

My sister's father-in-law suffered a mild heart attack on Super Bowl Sunday. He's in intensive care undergoing tests to uncover the cause. They've already determined his kidney function is compromised and that the chemo he underwent this month for his colon cancer caused damage to his heart.

A very tough time approaches for the family. How do they know when to pursue more treatments? When does the priority become comfort rather than a cure?

It's so hard to know when to flip the switch.

I think of a family caregiver I knew a few years ago who left no stone unturned in trying to cure her mother's urinary tract infections. The family caregiver saw any doctor and specialist she could to help her 94-year-old mom. She repeatedly bundled up her bed-bound mom, transferred her into and out of the car so they could sit in doctors' offices waiting for the cure that could not come. No cure existed for her mom's UTIs, only comfort measures. Even worse, no doctor she encountered explained that. A few months after her mom's death, the family caregiver told me how much she regretted missing those opportunities she had to simply be with her mom. The business of searching for a non-existent cure took away her finite time with her mom.

I have a colleague who still searches for a cure for his caree. With each attempt to cure, his caree's condition worsens as adjusting the meds and dosages changes his behavior. More appointments, more attempts, more frustration. My colleague has doctors and specialists who continue to offer "solutions" because my colleague is hellbent on finding a cure. The obsession with the cure, though, sacrifices the potential peace of the day and the opportunity to enjoy each other's presence. The gift of the moment gets lost in our tunnel vision.

In that dark tunnel, we decide to battle when the war no longer wages. When we keep swinging the sword, we can't see that we're really battling our ego rather than a disease process. Our ego lies to us, telling us we can beat death, we can over-rule mortality. The battle which never ends is really our own battle with our own fears.

It is soooo hard to know when to flip the switch. It can be such a challenge to find doctors who will honestly tell us when our obsession with chances means we lose our choices. It's so hard to feel so vulnerable to our fears and to acknowledge the truth that we just hate—that life is limited regardless of our best, tireless efforts.

Yet, it's the only way we really gain time. When time feels limited, switching from the hunt for the cure to the desire to keep our caree comfortable gains us time. We're no longer wasting time with procedures, doctors and strangers. Instead, we're making time with those we love.

How do we know when to make the switch? We can only know when we dare to ask the most difficult questions and have the courage to listen to the most heartbreaking answers.

There's such great honor in ensuring our family members receive the best comfort possible during their life's end. It's how we win.

End-of-Life Care: Working Within the Laws of Nature

This is hard to hear, but important to know. When you care, you help a family member die well.

The process of helping someone to die well begins early on in your caregiving journey. It begins when you first hear a diagnosis or when you first notice that your mother just isn't able to keep up the house as well as she used to. Or, when you celebrate your grandmother's 95th birthday and wonder, Where did the time go?

Early on in your caregiving journey, you were proactive in your efforts. You focused on finding the best doctor, uncovering the best treatment option, and providing the best care, such as nutritious meals, helpful home health aides, appropriate social stimulation. Your efforts worked. For awhile. Then the laws of nature took over, causing further frailty, greater declines.

Once the laws of nature became too much, you looked to achieve the status quo, holding on to what's left for as long as possible. You encouraged your mother to continue folding laundry, singing show tunes, reading the Bible.

Then the laws of nature take over again and the status quo keeps moving down a notch. Your mom likes to watch you fold the laundry; she likes to listen to show tunes on tape but can no longer vocalize the words; she wants your husband to read from the Bible.

This is how you give a good death.

When the laws of nature really begin to win, you wind down, together.

You sit together, no words. You allow longer and longer periods of rest. You give in to the clock.

This is when you become proactive again. You're setting the stage for the last hours, putting into your motion your caree's last wishes.

You prepare your house. You keep fresh flowers, you buy your mother's favorite CD, you ask your husband to polish up his rendition of your mother's favorite tune on the piano. You prepare the relatives and friends, inviting and encouraging visits. You prepare yourself, sharing with your caree your favorite memories, saying the words that have been left unsaid for too long. You prepare your caree, allowing her to gain strength for her last trip.

You celebrate life as you join forces to complete your last, and most important, work. You do it well, as you've done throughout your caregiving journey.

(Wondering how you can best create a space for your caree during the last weeks and days? Our Certified Caregiving Consultants can offer ideas and suggestions so that you and your caree feel surrounded by support and love.)

Worrying That, in the End, You'll be Cheated

A few years ago, my uncle died. That afternoon, I spoke with my cousin, Kelly, who sounded shell-shocked as she spoke about the awfulness of missing her father's last moments. He died in the hospice unit shortly before Kelly and her mom arrived. Kelly replayed the events of the morning, railing that she should have left the house earlier, gotten out of bed as soon as the alarm went off, made her arrival at the hospice her first and only priority that morning.

Kelly had been there–emotionally, physically, spiritually–for her dad for many years. She was the kind of loving and caring daughter I can only aspire to be. And, yet, she felt like a failure, that she had let her father down, deserted him to manage alone. In essence, she felt let down by life. How unfair that the last moment left without her.

Another family caregiver also shared this same fear that something will happen to his partner while he's at work or out taking a walk or enjoying a bike ride. This worry that he'll miss what feels most important has been ruling his day, pulling him into house, trapping him.

It's completely understandable. We care and care and care and brace for bad news, hoping our family members will continue. Then we hear the news that time is limited. We weather that news only to be left without the detail we need the most--when that last moment will happen. If only we knew, then we could leave our calendar open, take a leave of absence from work, make sure everyone arrives on time to say farewell, organize that last special get-together.

But we don't get the expiration date. How do you live with the unknown?

A few suggestions:

1. Live in the moment rather than managing the future. The worry about what will happen takes you out of this moment, the most important moment you have. When you try to control the arrival of the future, you realize today departed without you.

2. Talk out your fears with your caree, if appropriate, or other family members or your support system. Unvoiced fears truly hold your heart.

When you let them out, you can better manage them while uncovering a solution you overlooked.

3. Plan special moments for every day, such as expressing gratitudes together in the morning and sharing favorite memories in the evening. You also can simply sit with each other, in quiet love for each other's space.

4. Talk out your day's priorities with an understanding support system. When you verbalize what you're trying to juggle, you'll better understand how to organize your day as well as what can be delegated and what can be eliminated. The day can feel like a jumble; talking it out can make sense of it.

5. Live. The death watch will take the life out of you. As much as feels right to you, take breaks for yourself. When your break is over, share what happened during your break with your caree. It's how you continue. As much as feels right for you and your caree, plan outings and adventures together, even if the adventure only happens on the television show or YouTube video you watch together. It's how you both live well.

6. Measure the importance of your journey over the many moments you shared rather than just the last one. It's the culmination of those moments that matter. If you put too much pressure on the last moment, you can minimize the importance of all the other moments. Your presence throughout the entire caregiving experience has been steadfast, dependable and unshakable. That's what's most important.

I've wondered why we don't know our final day and time. Why isn't death more like birth, when we have a much better idea of the birth day? I guess we don't know so that we keep trying to live life to its fullest, so that we don't give up too soon and so we treasure each moment because we don't know how many we have left.

On this caregiving journey, it's you and your caree. Together, you fight, battle, catch your second, third, fourth, fifth winds. Caregiving ends, sadly, with the final separation. As I explained to my cousin, Kelly, sometimes your caree needs to end the journey without you.

I often think of my aunt, who died in 1995. During her last week, my cousins, parents and I did all we could to keep her company so she could die with us rather than alone. Our constant company just made it so hard for my aunt to pass. Finally, a hospice nurse asked us to leave the room so my aunt could be alone. With the room to herself, my aunt passed, with one tear rolling down her cheek.

I've come to understand that she really wasn't alone, even though we stood outside her room. When we left the room, we made room for others who had passed before her to come and get her.

Our carees never die alone. Our purpose is to simply prepare, as much as we can, for the transition. It's not our job to control the timing of the transition. I believe the experience of caregiving at the end becomes like maintaining a VIP waiting room. We care for our carees, our VIPs in our houses that become like waiting rooms in life as the other side makes ready for them to arrive after life. We gently let go to give over the care of our caree to the other angels.

It's so hard to let go. That's why, sometimes, life takes care of it for us.

If the end happens without you, know that you didn't get cheated. You can rest in the knowledge that life just took your cue and continued your loving care with the help of the angels.

Mom Promised That to Me!

When my grandmother died, she left her entire estate to her oldest son, my Uncle Con. My father, the only other child, did not receive anything.

Leaving one and excluding the other would seem to create a situation ripe with ill will and bad feelings. On the contrary, my father was in full support of his mother's decision.

My uncle had been my grandmother's primary caregiver. My parents and I helped. But, my uncle and aunt bore the brunt of my grandmother's care, even during the difficult years when my grandmother's manipulation made your head spin. (During one hospitalization, my grandmother was prescribed an anti-depressant. The result changed my grandmother and, thankfully, our relationship with her.) My grandmother had expressed her desire for Uncle Con to receive her entire estate, including possessions and assets. After her death, my uncle and father calmly settled her estate.

We were lucky. The inheritance of possessions can become a game of power that can be used to settle old scores, reinforce favorites, dredge up old family disputes. Sometimes, the greatest disputes seem to happen over who gets the good dishes rather than the bank accounts.

As the primary family caregiver, you'll see it all with your caree's possessions. You already may have seen a glimpse of the relatives who want the things but don't want the responsibility of caregiving. You may find yourself asking, Why should George get so much of Mom's things when he's done so little?

What's fair when distributing a caree's possessions? How can you best handle discussions with your caree about how to dispense his or her personal possessions after his or her death? The following tips, adapted from *Who Gets Grandma's Yellow Pie Plate* by Marlene S. Stum, Ph.D., Department of Family Social Science, University of Minnesota Extension Service, can help:

1. Be clear about your own motives for raising the issue. What are your concerns, what do you want to have happen, and why? Before beginning a discussion, you may want to use a friend as a sounding board to express any frustration toward other family members you may feel. You'll want your discussion to focus on your caree's wishes, rather than any frustrations you may feel, no matter how just.

2. Look for natural opportunities to talk with your caree. For example, perhaps a friend or relative recently dealt with transferring personal possessions after a death or a move. Use that situation to introduce a discussion with your caree. Ask, "What would you have done if you were in that situation?"

3. Keep using "what if" questions during your discussion. For example, "Dad, what would you want to have happen with the things in the house if you and Mom were no longer able to live here?"

4. Remember that listening is the part of communication we too often forget. After asking questions, listen to the answer with an objective ear. Express empathy toward your caree by saying, "I know this is an upsetting topic. I'm worried we won't handle your matters as you'd like. What do you worry about?"

5. Recognize that family members will have differing feelings and opinions. Point the discussions toward discovering those agreements and disagreements. If the disagreements seem to cause a divide too great to overcome, consider involving a mediator or elder law attorney. An objective third-party can keep the conversation focused on the objectives, rather than on any hurt feelings.

6. Be willing to listen and talk when another family member raises the issue. The situation only becomes personal if you make it so.

7. Not speaking up means others will not know your opinions or feelings. Express your thoughts assertively and graciously.

You may find that, even with your best attempts, you have a houseful of possessions to divide after your caree's death. Keep in mind that fair division of possessions is almost impossible. But, a fair mechanism to divide the possessions can be used. Here are some ideas:

1. Hold a raffle. Each family member picks a number out of the hat. Each family member takes a turn selecting a possession based on the number he or she picks. If your brother, Rick, picks Number 1, then he selects first. Your sister, Sylvia, who picks Number 2, selects next, etc.

2. If more than one family member indicates they would like the same possession, then put the names of all interested parties in a hat. The selected name becomes the owner of the possession.

3. Sell all the possessions and divide the proceeds.

4. Take turns sharing a prized family possession; a family treasure like the family Bible, family piano or family jewelry spends five years with each sibling before moving on to the next sibling's home.

Resources
- Grandma's Yellow Pie Plate:
  www.extension.umn.edu/family/personal-finance/decision-making/who-gets-grandmas-yellow-pie-plate/
- National Academy of Elder Law Attorneys: www.naela.org
- *The Boomer Burden: Dealing with your parents lifetime accumulation of stuff* by Julie Hall

"For my part I know nothing with any certainty, but the sight of the stars makes me dream." ~ Vincent van Gogh

Stage VI:
The Godspeed Caregiver

My caregiving role has ended.

Who are you?

Your role as caregiver ended more than two years ago. You find yourself compelled to make a difference in the lives of other family caregivers. You share information readily with family caregivers in the earlier stages. Perhaps you start a business dedicated to helping family caregivers or you find a job in which you assist family caregivers. Maybe you just make it habit to smile at everyone because you know you could be smiling at a family caregiver in need. You treasure each relationship you have in your life, recognizing that each day and your good health should never be taken for granted.

Your Keyword: Treasure

--Treasure your dreams.

--Treasure your challenges which led to your opportunities and new skills.

--Treasure your opportunities to share lessons learned.

--Treasure memories of your caree.

Your Challenge

To integrate your former role as a family caregiver into your new life.

Your Purpose

To implement your lessons learned from your role as caregiver, from your caree and from your family members and friends. During this stage, which can last as long you wish, even your lifetime, you reap the benefits of your efforts.

Judy

Frank died after living in the nursing home for eight months. During those eight months, Judy found herself somewhat lost. She struggled to relate again to her friends, to enjoy the old hobbies and interests she used to enjoy. She eventually joined the support group for family members at the nursing home. She found the other family members in the same fate: trying to rebuild their lives. After she shared the story of the pyramid of disposable briefs, she discovered the caregivers turned to her for assistance.

Now Judy facilitates two support groups--one through the Stroke Club at her local hospital, and one through the nursing home at which Frank was a resident. In addition to her work as a facilitator, Judy has become the "home care guru," answering questions that other family caregivers have.

Judy feels grateful for the peace she has found. She sleeps well at night.

Andy

When Andy returns to work after his mother's funeral, he finds himself looking at his coworkers differently, his job differently, his life differently. He decides his job doesn't match his passion--website design--and takes a sabbatical in order to explore opportunities to start his own business.

He communicates with siblings when the mood strikes. Although he has a casual relationship with them, he appreciates that he has them in his life.

He keeps in touch with his coworkers, who contact him regularly with eldercare issues. Andy is often told: Thank you for listening. Your support means the world to me.

The world, to Andy, is so much bigger and better than he ever imagined.

As a "Godspeed Caregiver," what can you do?

1. Follow your dreams.
Make your goals a reality.

2. Family caregivers will look to you as a mentor and leader.
Allow family caregivers in earlier stages the same freedom to stumble and steady themselves that you had. When they ask, share your experiences with those currently in a caregiving experience. When you can, listen to those family caregivers with understanding and empathy. Your ability to hear their experiences without judging those experiences will be an invaluable gift you give.

A Stumble:
Underestimating the importance of your caregiving journey

A Steady:
Review your journals and diaries and then ask, How am I different today?

3. Treasure the memories you have of your caree.

Continue to remember your caree regularly through rituals, such as enjoying an ice cream cone in her honor on her birthday or by planting trees in his honor. Reading and reviewing your diary will be a great way to remember.

Your best memorial to your caree's memory is a life you build for yourself filled with healthy relationships, productive careers and joy and laughter.

4. An apple a day…

Your apples kept you going. Now, consider how you'll use them to create your future. How did your apples change? How did you change? What would you like to try next? Go for it. The world is your apple.

The Godspeed Caregiver
Your Reflections

In this stage, what are your goals?

—For you?

—For your family?

How will you achieve these goals?

Who can help you achieve these goals?

Ask Denise: Does Caregiving Ever End Well?

Dear Denise,

I have a burning question that came to me in the last couple weeks and I can't seem to dismiss it. I thought you may have some insight to offer. Does caregiving ever end well? I really am curious.

Signed,
Hoping for a Happy Ending

Dear Hoping,

I think we all can have a happy ending in all experiences. I think it's being open to a new way of defining a happy ending.

During a caregiving experience, we can hang a happy ending on a recovery, a cure, a treatment that ensures our caree lives. The difficult part of caregiving is that it ends with a death after we've spent so much time (years, really) trying to avoid death. And, yet, I've never met anyone who's lived forever. We all die.

I think even when death is the end we can have a happy ending. When we have few regrets, when we know we loved well, when we know we have wonderful memories to comfort us, we can have a happy ending.

We might believe that death steals our happy ending. I believe the biggest thief of our happy ending is denial. Denial keeps you stuck in the past, which means you miss out on the present. When you deny the inevitable, you lose the moments right in front of you, the right-now moment to connect, to witness, to share, to love, to be.

During a caregiving experience, how do you balance a hope that better will come against the reality that death will arrive? On a regular basis, communicate with your caree, with your family, with your support system and with health care providers you trust to tell you the truth. Ask health care professionals the tough questions like, "What can we expect to happen next month, next year?" Ask your caree the toughest question, "Given the prognosis, how do you want to live?" If your caree has a cognitive impairment, then your knowledge from past conversations about wishes will help you balance the scale.

Understanding the reality of a caregiving situation means you have discussions with your caree about end-of-life, about death and about your life after your caree's death. I am fortunate in that I spend time with former family caregivers and listen as they share regrets they now have. Most regrets involve denial rearing its ugly head. It's what fear takes and never gives back: The chance to have meaningful conversations, the opportunity to be, the wisdom to keep a healthy and realistic perspective.

We can have a happy ending every day during caregiving if we simply allow a new definition of a happy ending. A happy ending is showing up when you would rather hide. A happy ending is speaking up for what's right when your knees knock so much you shake. A happy ending is ensuring your caree's end-of-life wishes are followed, regardless of how scary that feels to you. A happy ending is swallowing your pride so you can be vulnerable, whether alone with yourself or in a crowded room of strangers. A happy ending is speaking with your caree about his or her fears as you disclose yours. A happy ending is understanding that a zealous desire to cheat death can rob you of life. A happy ending is letting go at the very moment you so hope you can hang on. A happy ending means you speak with your family members about your future and your end-of-life wishes. A happy ending means you respect your health and your blessings and you do all you can to keep them. A happy ending is trusting the cycle of life and believing in the sacredness of life and death and all that happens in between.

Of course, during these moments–when you face your fears, when you show your vulnerability, when you let go–you've reached your life's worst moments. With the gift of time, you will see these worst moments as your bravest.

Life gives us test runs every day to create happy endings. I've learned that my days' happiest endings involve being honest, composed, open-minded and steadfast in my purpose. When I'm a bully or irate or operating from tunnel vision or steered off course by another's purpose, I don't have a happy ending at the end of the day. I have regrets.

We all die. Living with a fear of death keeps us from living well. When we aren't afraid of death or our future, when we keep the faith, we can have a happy ending.

When we can sleep at night, we have a happy ending. We give ourselves that peace when we stay present in our reality, which means we remain courageous, forgiving and gracious. Think of all those family members and friends who disappeared because they said they were "too busy" or they prefer "to remember him when he was healthy." These excuses are simply code for: "OMG! I have no idea how to cope with this." Those who performed a disappearing act will most likely lose, or at least misplace, their happy endings.

A happy ending during caregiving involves tears and sadness and very lonely moments and all that comes with mourning and grieving. It's the absence of lots of regrets that will bring the happy.

A happy ending isn't about an external outcome. It's about our internal peace we receive when we know we did our best during a horribly challenging time. It's about moving through your autumn and winter seasons because you know spring will arrive. It's about looking back with pride at your bravest moments.

"Heroes take journeys, confront dragons, and discover the treasure of their true selves." ~ Carol Lynn Pearson

"It is good to have an end to journey toward; but it is the journey that matters, in the end." ~ Ursula K. LeGuin

Your Tools

Our Certified Caregiving Consultants have tools to help you where you are and where you are going. The tools include:

- Life-Right-Now Wheel, which helps you determine what's going well and what you'd like to change
- Six Stages Wheels, which helps you ask, find, receive, welcome, allow and treasure
- Break Inspiration Wheel, which uncovers what's too much right now
- Fatigue Wheel, which spotlights the source of your fatigue
- Forgiveness Wheel, which identifies where you are with forgiveness
- Help Inspiration Wheel, which pinpoints the kind of help you need
- Limits Wheel, which shows you when you need a break
- Replenish Wheel, which offers ideas to refill
- Support Wheel, which inspires you to find the right support
- Team Wheel, which helps you form a team
- Your Caring Personality, which spotlights your strengths and your gifts
- Your End-of-Life Environment, which helps you create the right space for you and your caree at your caree's end-of-life
- Your Stress, which determines the source of our stress and ways to combat the stress.

To access these tools and schedule a complementary session with a consultant, visit caregiving.com/tools to access the tools and meet our consultants.

You'll also find helpful webinars on CareGiving.com which provide additional support to the material covered in this book, including a series on coping with compassion fatigue. To watch our webinars, visit www.caregiving.com/caregiving-webinars.

Your Respite Resources

Check with these organizations to get help so you can take a break:

- Check with your local Area Agency on Aging to find out about programs which help you get a break. Visit www.n4a.org.

- Call the Department of Veterans Affairs National Caregiver Support Line at 1-855-260-3274. Visit www.caregiver.va.gov.

- Hospice offers a five-day respite benefit so the primary family caregiver can take a break.

- Contact your local assisted living facilities and nursing homes to learn about short-term placement for your caree.

- Alzheimer's and Dementia Care Relief Grant Program, created by Hilarity for Charity, offers in-home help to give you a break. Visit hilarityforcharity.org/programs/grant-program.

- Disease-specific organizations, like the Alzheimer's Association and ALS Association, may offer respite programs.

- Search for help through ARCH National Respite Network and Resource Center. Visit archrespite.org/index.php.

- Easter Seals offers programs for adults and children with disabilities. Visit www.easterseals.com.

- National Association of Adult Day Services may offer services to help you take a break. Visit www.nadsa.org.

- National Volunteer Caregiving Network may have volunteers who can help. Visit www.nvcnetwork.org.

- Shepherd's Centers of America offer volunteer caregiving services. Visit www.shepherdcenters.org.

- Volunteers of America may have a volunteer who can give you a break. Visit www.voa.org/get-help.

Your Resources

Administration for Community Living: www.acl.gov

Aging Life Care Association: www.aginglifecare.org

American Association of Daily Money Managers:
https://secure.aadmm.com

Benefits CheckUp: www.benefitscheckup.org
Search to learn about services that may help.

Center for Medicare Advocacy: www.medicareadvocacy.org
Offers help with Medicare appeals.

ElderCare Locator: 800-677-1116
Call for help connecting to your local Area Agency on Aging.

Financial Planning Association: www.plannersearch.org

Leading Age: www.leadingage.org/find-member
Search for aging services and providers.

Medicaid: www.medicaid.gov

Medicare: www.medicare.gov

My Medicare Matters: www.mymedicarematters.org
Helps you choose a Medicare plan.

National Academy of ElderLaw Attorneys: www.naela.org

National Library of Medicine: www.nlm.nih.gov

National Association for Home Care and Hospice: www.nahc.org

National Association of Senior Move Managers: www.nasmm.org

National Aging and Disability Transportation Center: www.nadtc.org

Next Step in Care website: www.nextstepincare.org
Get guides and checklists to help when your caree transitions between care settings such as from the hospital to home.

Social Security Administration: www.ssa.gov

Additional Resources

As you research help for you and your caree, consider both help you hire and help you receive from volunteers, including:

- Meals on Wheels
- Telephone check-in services
- Home health agencies
- Neighbors
- Aging Life Care Specialists
- Snow removal services
- Lawn maintenance services
- Cleaning services
- Grocery delivery services
- Local teenagers
- Local university students, including those majoring in pre-med or nursing
- Elderlaw attorney
- Financial planner
- Pharmacist
- Geriatrician
- Personal emergency response systems
- Community programs such as parish nurses and social service agencies
- House of worship
- Family Medical Leave Act so you can take an unpaid leave from work
- Employee Assistance Program through your employer
- Disease-specific groups, such as the Alzheimer's Association and Alzheimer's Foundation of America, for support groups and referrals to help
- The mail carrier who can bring mail to the door if your caree has a long walk to the mailbox
- Certified Caregiving Consultants
- Others who've been through something similar like members of CareGiving.com, who can be a terrific resource for you.

Your Take-Away

Your caregiving journey is first about your caree, then about you and your caree together, then just about you. When it's just about you, you decide, you choose, you become.

Become your dream.

About the Author

Denise M. Brown, Professional Caregiving Coach and Speaker, began working with family caregivers in 1990. She was an early developer of online support groups for family caregivers and former family caregivers, launching her first in 1996 through her website, CareGiving.com. Through her website, seminars, books and coaching practice, Denise helps family caregivers and former family caregivers find meaning in their caregiving and after-caregiving journeys.

Denise hosts the National Caregiving Conference every November in Chicago. You also can watch the conference virtually.

Denise developed the Certified Caregiving Consultant and Educator programs to empower and train former family caregivers to guide today's family caregivers.

To reach Denise, please visit CareGiving.com.